MAKING THE
CISCO
CONNECTION

MAKING THE CISCO CONNECTION

THE STORY BEHIND THE REAL **INTERNET SUPERPOWER**

DAVID BUNNELL

CEO/EDITOR, UPSIDE MEDIA, WITH ADAM BRATE

John Wiley & Sons, Inc.

New York • Chichester • Weinheim • Brisbane • Singapore • Toronto

Published by John Wiley & Sons, Inc.
Published simultaneously in Canada.

This publication is designed to provide accurate and authoritative information in regard to the subject matter covered. It is sold with the understanding that the publisher is not engaged in rendering legal, accounting, or other professional services. If legal advice or other expert assistance is required, the services of a competent professional person should be sought.

Designations used by companies to distinguish their products are often claimed as trademarks. In all instances where John Wiley & Sons, Inc. is aware of a claim, the product names appear in initial capital or all capital letters. Readers, however, should contact the appropriate companies for more complete information regarding trademarks and registration.

ISBN 0-471-35711-1

Printed in the United States of America.

10 9 8 7 6 5 4 3 2 1

Contents

Foreword

In late 1999, Cisco Systems usurped venerable Intel's place as the most valuable company in Silicon Valley. Then, a few weeks shy of its fifteenth birthday on December 10, 1999, Cisco became only the third company in history (following General Electric and Microsoft) to burst past the $300 billion mark in market capitalization. And yet, Cisco, based in San Jose, California, remains relatively unknown compared to its peers. Its products, networking equipment such as routers and hubs, do not generate the instant recognition that Microsoft's Windows or Intel's microprocessors do. This book—which describes Cisco's history, its ambitious expansion plans, and its unique acquisition strategy—should help catapult Cisco to the place it deserves among business success stories.

Two years ago, when I was writing *Silicon Gold Rush*, which included Cisco among two dozen technology companies I explored as emblems of a new way of doing business, I was already impressed by Cisco's rapid ascent to greatness. Certainly its two founders, Leonard Bosack and Sandy Lerner, who were attending Stanford University, happened to be in the right place at the right time. Silicon Valley in the mid-1980s was at the center of the computer revolution. When Bosack and Lerner devised a way to solve a growing problem—allowing disparate computer networks to communicate via their electronic router—a market quickly developed. Bosack and Lerner, who later married and are now divorced, turned to venture capital, another Silicon Valley institution that had grown up alongside the computer industry, to fund their little start-up. Sequoia Capital's Don Valentine invested $2.5 million in 1986 and reaped $10 billion when Cisco went public the following year.

But Cisco is not a success merely because it invented a hot new technology and made a lot of investors and employees very, very rich. In that it was following in the footsteps of other Silicon Valley pioneers, like Intel, Apple, and Sun Microsystems. What is especially impressive about Cisco is how it has managed to achieve its sizzling growth and to dominate the networking industry even in the face of formidable competition. While companies like Microsoft and Intel had the advantage early on of being handed a near monopoly by IBM, Cisco had no such jump-start. From the beginning it faced competitors such as 3Com and Cabletron, and convincingly trounced them all. Today, it is defiantly challenging much bigger competitors (in terms of revenue) that have moved into networking from the telephony equipment market—Lucent and Nortel. Still, the fact that Cisco's market cap is third highest in the country, while its sales place it at only 192 on the Fortune 500 list, tells you what investors continue to expect from this streaking company.

In the 1990s, Cisco did two things that kept it among the leaders of the technology revolution, while many other pioneers slipped: It developed a once-derided, now-renowned strategy of *innovation by acquisition,* and it correctly identified the Internet as the wave of the future and leaped on top.

Before Cisco, new technology powerhouses such as Intel and Apple, and old players such as IBM, prided themselves on their ability to innovate from within. The not-invented-here syndrome was rampant in the industry—if something new wasn't created by your own internal teams, it couldn't be worth much. Cisco turned that adage on its head. Realizing that the networking market in which it operated was evolving far too rapidly for any one company, no matter how big or inventive, to keep up, Cisco used its appreciating stock as currency to launch an unprecedented acquisition drive. It took over mostly small companies—some barely more than research teams—that had technology it could enfold and leverage with its formidable distribution network. Thanks in large part to Cisco, acquisition became as acceptable an exit strategy as an IPO for technology start-ups. Not only that, established technology companies had to abandon the not-invented-here philosophy or be left behind by the ever-acquisitive Cisco, which has now snapped up dozens of companies.

John Chambers is Cisco's third CEO, but he is the one who indelibly stamped it as an Internet company. After taking over in 1994, he moved quickly to position Cisco's networking capabilities to satisfy the Internet's insatiable appetite for communications systems that would link its millions of users. Today, Chambers has an even grander vision, as the Internet becomes part of a global communications network that encompasses wireless and wired communications, satellites, and telephones. Cisco hopes its Internet prowess will enable it to become a central hub in this worldwide network, as Marshall McLuhan's global village finally becomes a reality.

Cisco's journey, as depicted in this book, is a fascinating account of a company that invented a new technology and reinvigorated a once-denigrated business strategy. The journey is filled with eccentric, colorful, innovative characters, like Bosack, Lerner, Chambers, Valentine, and former CEO John Morgridge. If you join in, you'll learn how Cisco enfolds acquired companies in a way that maintains their own innovative abilities, and how it has managed to avoid much of the animosity that dominance usually brings. Cisco's eclectic culture, defined as "a solid core and fuzzy edges" by one of its human resource directors, deserves to be studied as an example of how a leading-edge company embraces and leads change. If you want to understand how the successful twenty-first century business model might evolve, Cisco is a good place to start.

Karen Southwick
Executive Editor, *Forbes ASAP*
Author of *Silicon Gold Rush*
and *High Noon*

Preface

Cisco Systems is known among the technology elite of Silicon Valley as one of the most successful companies to emerge from the Valley in many years. Some industry analysts have even dubbed it computing's next superpower. And at the time of this writing, Cisco has captured the top spot in the market-cap race among Silicon Valley companies, overtaking Intel.

Just as Intel and Microsoft soared to lofty heights with the rise of the personal computer, Cisco Systems is flying on the spectacular updraft of the Internet. The company has captured 85 percent of the market for routers, which are used as the backbone for the biggest network of them all, the Internet. As a result, over the last five years, the value of Cisco's total outstanding stock has risen more than 2,000 percent—twice the increase of Microsoft Corporation's stock in the same period.

The Cisco story is a very unusual tale of corporate success. Despite the struggle of passing through several regimes, Cisco managed to hit all the sweet spots of its business and consistently bested competitors like 3Com and IBM with insight, innovation, customer focus, and one of the biggest corporate buying sprees in history.

Through conversations my colleagues and I have had with Cisco's management, as well as with industry analysts and researchers, which are reflected in this book, I hope to explain how Cisco has become synonymous with the Internet. Cisco has successfully moved beyond producing Internet routers and established itself as a global communications giant. *Making the Cisco Connection* deftly traces the networking giant's path to success. It highlights the company's incisive strategy for acquiring niche technology makers and competitors, making them part of a huge community with its own highly developed use of technology and an unusually tight-knit culture. Cisco shines with a kinder, gentler image, emphasizing happy customers and employees. You'll see how Cisco built its impressive culture by cultivating community, boosting morale, whittling down bureaucracy, and saving money to boot.

Making the Cisco Connection traces the unique history of one of the most profitable and enduring technology companies in business today. The result is a thought-provoking portrait of an organization that is on the way to becoming one of the most influential companies of our time.

Acknowledgments

This book was realized with the help of a number of journalists who worked with me to assemble the perspectives and experiences featured in this book. I would like to thank the contributions made by Karen Southwick, Paul Franson, Eric Nee and the Upside staff, as well as the untiring efforts of Richard Brandt. In addition to offering his expert analysis on Cisco's place in the high-tech marketplace, Richard has been the strongest advocate for the book and devoted many hours to researching and arranging for interviews. Finally, I would like to thank my editor, Jeanne Glasser, and the entire Wiley team who, in the true spirit of collaboration, brought this book to fruition.

Introduction

On August 25, 1999, John Chambers, the CEO of Cisco Systems, made a stunning announcement. Cisco had reached an agreement to buy a small network equipment company called Cerent Corporation. A *tiny* company. Just two years old, its products were barely on the market. In order to land this prize, Chambers offered Cerent's shareholders 100 million shares of Cisco stock. At that time, it made the purchase price a whopping $7 billion.

Now, on the one hand, this deal made a lot of sense. Chambers had huge ambitions to make Cisco the architect of a new worldwide communication system for the twenty-first century, and Cerent had a really nifty piece of technology that could help. Just eight months earlier, this hot little two-year-old had introduced its first product: equipment that could take bits of data from the old copper-wire telephone networks and launch them onto state-of-the-art fiber-optic networks, the communications superautobahn for the next millennium. Cerent's products had won rave reviews, and the company had already been listed as an up-and-comer by *Forbes* and *Business Week*.

But *$7 billion?* Cerent might have sold $50 million worth of equipment in its entire lifetime, if it was lucky. In addition to spending about 140 times Cerent's lifetime revenues to date, Chambers offered the executives of this pipsqueak company senior positions at $12 billion Cisco and guaranteed that no one from Cerent would be fired without approval from Cerent's CEO. Which begs the question: *Is this guy crazy?*

Perhaps. It wouldn't be the first time Wall Street and the press questioned, shall we say, the rationality of Chambers's decisions. Two years earlier, he had spent $4.4 billion on another small company called StrataCom. His competitors still laugh at that one, and some Wall Street analysts still wonder whether he got his money's worth.

But a little bit of craziness can take a company a long way in today's world. And there is a little bit of magic to this madness. By staying ahead of his competition, making some savvy acquisitions, and executing the proper marketing and public relations acrobatics, Chambers has managed to associate his company's image strongly with the Internet. The stock-buying frenzy that has seized all things Internet has seized Cisco as well. In the past 5 years, the value of Cisco's total outstanding stock has risen over 2,000 percent—twice the increase of Microsoft Corporation stock in the same period.

This gives Chambers incredible wealth to play with. He can afford to buy overvalued companies, because he is paying for them with his own overvalued stock. He's not using cash, he's using what industry wags refer to as "Cisco dollars." This currency keeps increasing in value relative to government-issued dollars daily. This is the same method used by such technology leaders as MCI/WorldCom and Microsoft.

Cisco is at the forefront of one of the greatest technology and business shifts this country has ever known. The growth of the Internet has become an extraordinary landslide that is sweeping most of the business world along with it. Those companies that can ride it out will see the potential for untold wealth once the mud settles. Those who cannot will be buried. Add to this the fact that the U.S.

telephone system is struggling through the throes of deregulation, trying to adapt to the changes the Internet brings, and trying to go global, and it is apparent that timidity is not the way to get ahead.

Especially not if you're running Cisco. The company sells specialized computer equipment that routes traffic through the Internet, and has already grown phenomenally with the Internet's rise. Cisco has become known as the company building the Internet's foundation. When Chambers joined Cisco in 1991 (he was made CEO in 1994), the company had annual sales of just $70 million. Cisco should pass $16 billion in sales for the fiscal year ending July 31, 2000.

But the Internet is not enough for Chambers. He believes that all the world's communications systems, from telephones, television, and radio broadcasts to satellites, wireless systems, and the Internet, will converge into a single giant, global communications system. When it happens—in just a few short years—Chambers wants to be able to ride that landslide, too, and emerge not just as one of the world's top corporations, but (as he recently boasted to *Business Week*) "one of the most influential companies in history."

■ NOT YOUR FATHER'S OLD WORLD COMPANY

There is only one problem. This is not a one-horse race. By moving beyond Internet routers in an attempt to create a huge convergent global network, Cisco is entering a new, competitive playing field. It is now challenging players several times its size, such as AT&T spinoff Lucent Technologies, Canada's Nortel networks, Germany's Siemens, and Japan's Fujitsu.

Just as Microsoft took on IBM in the computer business, and just as the growing company now called MCI/World-

Com is taking on the established phone companies, so too is Cisco the newcomer in the field of communications networks, the hotshot riding the momentum of the Internet.

This edge makes Cisco, the new kid in the neighborhood, just a bit arrogant. Chambers is fond of describing his competitors as "Old World" companies that will lose out to his "New World" order. He raises the ire of some of his biggest customers, the giant telephone companies, by brashly insisting to anyone who will listen that within a few years, all long-distance phone calls will be free. Lack of boldness is not a problem.

But exactly what is this New World culture? Companies like Intel and Microsoft clearly represent New World thinking. And, indeed, Cisco is sometimes compared to those companies, including the amount of clout its huge market share brings. Some 80 percent of the routers directing data through the Internet come from Cisco.

But Cisco's culture is harder to define that those of either Microsoft or Intel. While those companies are known to be ruthless competitors, and have both been investigated by the federal government for allegedly abusing their near-monopolies in their fields, Cisco's public image is almost touchy-feely. Cisco is not only New World, it's almost New Age—at least in image. It is not only hugely egalitarian, like most of the rest of Silicon Valley (even the most senior executives sit inside the same Dilbert cubicles as everyone else), it promotes an almost overly friendly image of corporate fairness. Hence, Cisco's rule of never laying off employees from companies it acquires without the permission of the acquired company's former CEO. Chambers is known for his inspirational sermonlike rallies to fire up his troops and monthly "birthday breakfasts" to which any Cisco employee having a birthday that month is invited. Employees are given a plastic card listing the corporate values— mostly exhortations to always put customers first and to play fair—to attach to their company ID cards and carry with them constantly.

Chambers also claims to be an advocate of "coopetition," or working together with competitors, sometimes even giving up lucrative business if it would serve the customer better. He claims he would never want a monopoly like Microsoft's because the competition makes Cisco better.

Even the company's employees sometimes don't know how much of that to believe. Most seem to be Cisco loyalists and take Chambers at his word. They are most likely right. And yet, Chambers's competitors also grouse that he has been known to strong-arm competitors who threaten to buy competing gear, because they are so dependent on Cisco. The Federal Trade Commission even investigated one of Chambers's attempts at coopetition when he approached Lucent and Nortel about the possibility of working together instead of competing head-on in certain areas. The Feds were suspicious that it could amount to collusion, but dropped the case soon after.

Of course, these executives may also be just a bit jealous of Chambers's ability to make Cisco seem like the coolest kid in the neighborhood. And they definitely bristle at his characterization of their businesses as Old World companies. But it's not all merely spin and polish. "There's a lot to what Chambers says," asserts Dave House, who was CEO at Cisco competitor Bay Networks until it was acquired in 1998 by Nortel. House is in a good position to know. After competing with Cisco for several years, he is now taking his wealth from the Nortel acquisition and retiring. Nortel and Lucent "have to learn to make decisions quicker, become more Silicon Valley–like," says House. "Because Chambers is good, and Cisco is good."

On the other hand, Cisco still has a few tricks to learn itself. While Cisco is an expert in the technology that runs the Internet, a lot of other technology will be involved in this huge convergence, as well. Lucent and Nortel, two of the largest suppliers of telephony equipment, also have considerable technological expertise. They are particularly strong in fiber-optic technology, for example. That's why Chambers has been on a mad shopping spree over the last few years for small companies with new technology, and why he sometimes seems willing to pay almost any price to get something he deems critical—such as Cerent's own fiber-optic expertise.

In addition, Cisco lacks the reliability of the old phone networks, its competitors' relationships with the big phone companies, their huge service and support staffs, and even the ability to help customers finance their purchases. "There's a lot Cisco doesn't have," adds House.

The race is barely out of the starting gate, and it is impossible to give anyone the early lead. But like all things Internet, this race will be a fast one. The winners will become clear in a few short years, and the world will be transformed in the process.

■ WHO'S RUNNING THIS SHOW?

But it is Cisco that makes the race really interesting—not only for its bold strategy, but for the colorful cast of characters who have been in charge over the years. Amazingly, unlike Microsoft, which has been guided by Chairman Bill Gates's firm hand from the start, Cisco's control has shifted from one regime to another without losing momentum.

Chambers himself hates to read. He insists that a huge number of executives report to him personally and deliver their reports verbally and in person. All for good reason: He's dyslexic. Furthermore, before finding phenomenal success at Cisco, he experienced phenomenal failure at his previous companies, IBM and Wang Laboratories, which were being battered at the time by the personal computer revolution. At Wang, Chambers mostly found himself overseeing layoffs as the company slowly receded into bankruptcy.

Before Chambers came along, Cisco had the most unusual mix of executives in Silicon Valley. The company got its start in the computer labs at Stanford University, founded by two lovers with a rare and eccentric mix of talents—business school graduate Sandra Lerner and computer scientist Leonard Bosack (they were later married, and then divorced). The idea of an MBA and a nerd in love is such an incongruity that their story became a legend in Silicon Valley.

Toss one of Silicon Valley's most prominent venture capitalists, Don Valentine, into the mix, and you've got a potentially explosive mix of personalities. And, indeed, Cisco has had its share of internal strife. And yet, the company has managed to defy all conventional wisdom and end up (so far) on top.

In the end—who knows?—conventional wisdom could prove right. Perhaps Cisco, which alone in the Valley has managed to find enormous growth by stringing together some very clever small companies, will someday burst at the seams. But no matter what happens, it will prove to be one of the most unusual business stories of the Internet generation.

Chapter

The Truth behind the
Cisco Legend (1984–1987)

■ COMPATIBILITY ISSUES ■ REAL ROOTS OF THE ROUTER
■ AN UNAUTHORIZED SANCTION ■ GREEN INFANT CISCO
■ GETTING FUNDED ■ A SEED IN SILICON VALLEY

The Cisco legend is the tale of two inhibited sweethearts at Stanford University in the late 1970s. Sandra Lerner of the Stanford University Business School and Leonard Bosack of the computer science department wanted to send love letters to each other via e-mail, but their respective departments used different computer networks. So Len and Sandy, impassioned and determined, invented the router—a mysterious black box consisting of a twist of cable and some agile software. Then they conceived Cisco. The router made Cisco the fastest-growing company ever. In 1999, 15 years after its founding, Cisco was worth $200 billion.

The Cisco legend, as it exists in the annals of high-tech history, reflects all the qualities of effective hyperbole: It involves love, a faceless enemy, a victory, and easy money.

1

Incidentally, it's somewhat deceptive. A backbone of truth, however remains: Len and Sandy *were* a bona fide couple at Stanford, they *did* found Cisco, and, most truly, the networking giant *did* achieve record-breaking growth that enabled it to consummate a high-tech tryst with Microsoft and Intel. Like searching the Web itself, telling the *actual* Cisco story involves tracking a couple of key characters and tracing a few infinitely connected links.

■ COMPATIBILITY ISSUES

Sandy and Len met in 1977, when Sandy was a graduate student and Len was a computer nerd who shared time on the minicomputers at the Low Overhead Time Sharing System (LOTSS) building of the Stanford computer science department. The name of the facility itself suggests one of the problems that networked personal computers would solve—users having to share very scarce, centralized systems. The vast majority of the comp sci students using the LOTSS were men, a clan that by all accounts was poignantly unconcerned with personal hygiene. Of all the geeks who hung out there, Len (once described by a reporter as looking like a "very tidy little bartender") was the one who bathed and washed his collars and cuffs. Sandy later claimed she was enchanted with Len because he actually knew how to bathe and ate with silverware. Sandy likewise practiced good hygiene, and the two discovered that they also had keen intelligence and a sense of humor in common. Other than that, the two were, personality-wise, polar opposites. Len, a University of Pennsylvania electrical-engineering major with a Stanford master's degree in computer science, was known as the philosophical and nonconfrontational one. Sandy, an economics major working for a master's in statistics and computer science (or, as she deemed it, "sadistics and confusing science"), was notoriously extravagant and aggressive. Abiding by the law that opposites attract, the couple married after a high-speed courtship and continued their parallel careers at Stanford.

By the time 1979 rolled around, the computer industry was on the cusp of upheaval. Though few dared to predict it at the time, IBM's days as king of computing with its mainframes and minicomputers were numbered. Supercheap personal computers from companies like Apple and Tandy were starting to erode the minicomputer dominance of IBM, Hewlett-Packard, and Digital Equipment Corporation (DEC). Ethernet and TCP/IP were ready for action. The formative elements of the Internet—the Advanced Research Project Agency network's Interface Message Processors (ARPAnet IMPs)—which connected computer clusters at Stanford and other universities to their respective ARPAnets, had spread like wildfire despite their limited capacities. As computer scientists, Len and Sandy were entering a new, volatile era.

After graduating, Sandy became director of the computer facilities at Stanford University Business School. Len, at the time, was director of Stanford's computer science department. Back in 1982, the Stanford campus housed a total of about 5,000 different computers. Like the Tower of Babel, the scores of computers on the sweeping campus failed to "talk" effectively to one another beyond limited ranges. Each Stanford building may have supported a self-contained network—clusters could talk to one another and e-mail could be sent to other universities via ARPAnet—but students couldn't apply research conducted on a computer in one department to their paper that resided in another. To get computers to share information, data traffic would be passed up to the ARPAnet from a local network, broadcast across the net, and then received at an ARPAnet IMP terminal in another building.

The locally networked computers could only access the ARPAnet through the IMP machines, which, incidentally, cost more than $100,000 apiece. It was obvious to Len and Sandy and others that local data could be transmitted more quickly, reliably, and safely by bypassing the ARPAnet altogether—but no such solution existed. If the IMP broke down, students would have to save data on tape or 5-inch floppy disks and trundle it over to the next computer—a method wryly called "sneaker-net." Typifying the tribulations of network managers like Len and Sandy, the campus supported more than 20 incompatible e-mail systems. Len and Sandy had to manage not only the central departmental computers, but also the networks and, in Len's case, computers using the Ethernet network, as well. They needed to find some way to get the local computers networked.

■ REAL ROOTS OF THE ROUTER

Sandy and Len have tried to dispel the popular myth that they invented the router, the black box that transmits and translates data to and from disparate computers. "Len and I did not invent the router," Sandy asserted. "No way. We did not invent terminal servers and we did not invent Ethernet interfaces and we did not invent Ethernet. Or TCP/IP or any of that."[1] But the couple was a catalyst for the router's implementation.

The real story behind Len and Sandy's router hearkens back to Christmas Day, 1979. Santa Claus came to Stanford University (as well as MIT and Carnegie-Mellon) in the guise of the Xerox Palo Alto Research Campus (Xerox PARC), toting the latest in technological innovations: Altos computers and 3-megabyte (MB) Ethernet equipment. The Stanford Medical School and the computer science department each quickly used the equipment to install separate networks, which were some of the earliest local-area networks (LANs) in the world. Other departments, like the Stanford University Business School, had DEC minicomputers. The urge to connect the networks between buildings preceded Len and Sandy.

Ralph Gorin, manager of LOTSS, was one of the people who had spent several years working to connect the discrete networks. The Stanford University networking specialists constructed *bridges,* which operated at the data-link layer, to extend networks. The bridges worked well with ARPAnet and the IMPs, but not for hooking up local computers on the Stanford campus. For the networks to be truly interconnected, routers that could deal with the local-area protocols were necessary. Routers, unlike bridges, would allow the two LANs to remain distinct, while being able to communicate.

An engineer named Bill Yeager, who was in the Stanford Medical School, was assigned to design the routers. By June 1980, he developed a crude router based on a DEC minicomputer that connected the medical school and computer science department networks. Len Bosack was especially suited to setting up the router. He had worked on its predecessor, the PDP-10, as an engineer at Digital Equipment Corporation in the 1970s. The router was a brilliant idea with great commercial potential. At the time, networking was beginning to invade corporate America. A great deal of money and resources were being pumped into network research and development. Eric Benhamou and married couple Judith Estrin and William Carrico founded Bridge Networks and built equipment (especially bridges) for enterprise LANs. 3Com began selling Ethernet cards for Intel's personal computers, which would connect them to Ethernet networks. The Stanford University Network (SUN) project had been trying to construct a multimillion-dollar high-speed cross-campus Ethernet network, with workstations that could run the Unix operating system. In 1982, however, none of these efforts was fully effective in getting Stanford interconnected. So Sandy and Len and a group of colleagues decided to experiment.

■ AN UNAUTHORIZED SANCTION

The Stanford experimenters—Len, Sandy, and other Stanford engineers, including Kirk Lougheed—working without permission or an official budget, first created the interface by which they could connect the DEC minicomputers to a bootleg Ethernet network. The network consisted of a few miles of coaxial cable—the same kind of wiring that delivers cable television service—that they ran between the buildings on the 15-odd square mile campus. The guerrilla team pulled wires through manholes, and sewer pipes—everywhere that made sense. They spent innumerable hours setting up the routers, servers, and other computers to communicate with one another and the ARPAnet/Internet.

While they laid down wires and installed boxes, others were working on the software. Yeager began adding code for the Stanford routers that would allow them to coordinate the network more effectively. This would later become a primitive network operating system. Other Stanford coders, like Jeff Mogul, Steve Nowicki, and Benjy Levy, extended and improved the operating system to include a host of network services.

The project was a success. The router enabled the connection of normally incompatible individual networks. It allowed data to be read by any computer in the network, even across different operating systems. Soon enough, the bootleg system became the official Stanford University Network.

Len and Sandy cleared space in their living room for the design and manufacture of more black boxes that would be tested on Stanford's network. The word about these boxes spread like wildfire by e-mail over ARPAnet within Stanford and to other universities and research centers that were soon knocking on Stanford's gates in an effort to buy them.

Len and Sandy's grassroots efforts on the campus grounds were hardly approved by the university. Sandy later told *Fortune* magazine that, "We crammed it down Stanford's throat."[2] The couple went to Stanford's administration with a proposal to design and build routers under the school's aegis for sale to colleagues and businesses, but Stanford refused. They had recently failed to capitalize— really, to profit at all—on Sun Microsystems' success (although they got name credit, since Sun stands for the original Stanford University Network project). The Office of Technology Licensing (OTL) had allowed student Andy Bechtolsheim to take off with his Sun workstation technology. Although the OTL was cognizant of the opportunity the couple had offered, they were unable to take any action to support the development of Len and Sandy's router business in any time less than a year or two. Rather than lose face again as they had with Sun, Stanford felt it was better to let some other company forge the router industry. After all, the university was not in the business of manufacturing and selling technology. The decision makers did not give Len and Sandy permission to continue their business on campus or to use school resources for making routers for colleagues at Xerox Labs and Hewlett-Packard.

Livid, the couple decided to gather up their technology, quit their jobs, and leave Stanford to start their own business. Speculation has it that Cisco never would have existed if Stanford hadn't tried to clip Len and Sandy's wings.

■ GREEN INFANT CISCO

In late 1984, Len and Sandy financed their own start-up costs with their credit cards, boosted by technology they borrowed (or, some say, took) from Stanford. Sandy dubbed their brand new business "cisco (with a lowercase *c*, as in the tail of San Fran) Systems." The couple worked split shifts to get it off the ground. Sandy designed the logo in the form of the Golden Gate Bridge—Cisco's insignia to this day. Sandy and Len had settled on "cisco" with their lawyers after extensive searches. Although the food-service provider Sysco was in business at the time, "cisco" did not conflict with them or any other business, and the lowercase variant was made official. (The current name, "Cisco," remained "cisco" for several years. Factions within and external to the company adopted a capital *C* despite the determined efforts of traditionalists. The company logo now emphasizes "Cisco" with an uppercase initial letter.)

Len and Sandy mortgaged their house for additional capital, and Sandy took a job with Schlumberger, an international technical company, in addition to working for cisco. The couple transformed their living room at 199 Oak Grove Avenue, Atherton (now a wealthy enclave of Silicon Valley), into the headquarters for the design and manufacture of networking technology. Their modest home became a place where friends like Stanford engineers Kirk Lougheed, Greg Satz, and Richard Troiano would come over to write code, piece together boxes, and assemble cables. Soon, the project snaked out from the bedroom to the living room and every other room in the house as the group tested the prototypes of new routers. As Len remembers, the interminable work became a true gauge of stamina and dedication, with "sincerity" beginning when an employee spent more than 100 hours a week working. After the 100-hour-per-week point, the situation became reminiscent of the LOTSS lab, requiring the cisco employees to regiment the rest of their lives by eating once a day and showering every other day. When employees worked beyond 110 hours per week, according to Len, they weren't just sincere, they were "committed."

In 1986, cisco moved to its own office space on 1360 Willow Road in Menlo Park. With the move, Lougheed, Satz, and Troiano left Stanford to officially help Sandy and Len build cisco. Cisco had licensed Bill Yeager's original router code, and Kirk Lougheed stripped it and improved its Internet Protocol (IP) support. He also made other critical improvements that brought the software much closer to being viable as a commercial product. In 1987, cisco began shipping the unique software and hardware package they called, with typical nerdlike efficiency, a "cisco."

From the start, cisco Systems focused on maintaining a unique relationship with its customers. In the mid-1980s the company had no professional sales staff or official marketing campaign (indeed, Cisco did not purchase its first advertisement until 1992). In what might be considered some of the earliest spam (and a violation of the rules of the National Science Foundation, which "owned" the ARPAnet/Internet at the time), Sandy and Len fired out commercial e-mails to friends and colleagues, encouraging them to spread the message to others over the Web's early links. Cisco guessed on pricing, and charged anywhere between $7,000 to $50,000 per router to universities and big corporations desperate to unite their disparate computers. Despite the immoderate price and lack of dazzle, Cisco turned a profit of $250,000 to $350,000 a month on network servers as early as 1986. Sandy and Len kept the phone near their bed to answer the 4-A.M. calls. Business was booming. A self-proclaimed socialist since the age of 12, Sandy quipped to a reporter at *Forbes* that, "It was not my intention to get rich. My intention was not to be poor."[3]

Sandy and Len learned what the marketplace needed by letting their customers be partners—a business strategy that has only recently been adopted by mainstream businesses. Cisco didn't just sell ciscos to their customers; they also let customers tinker with the source code that ran the ciscos. In fact, one early customer, Chuck Hendrick at Rutgers University, added DECnet routing to code (DECnet routing was independent of IP routing). Similarly, Greg Satz added another protocol, called XNS routing, back into the code. Through these various evolutions and adaptations, the multiprotocol router that we use today emerged.

■ GETTING FUNDED

By 1987, when other networking companies began to sprout up, Cisco Systems had reached the point at which it had to grow much, much bigger in its market share and profitability or risk a plateau and plummet. Credit cards were no longer the funding of choice—and the 110-hour standard for "commitment" didn't cut it. Sandy and Len were compelled to find alternative means of support—namely, venture capital (VC). The pair pitched their company and product to 75 VC firms without success. With irony, Sandy later confided that at least 70 of them were pretty convinced that the pair was crazy. Eventually, Don Valentine, founder and general partner at Sequoia Systems, agreed to front the money—$2.5 million dollars—for a 32 percent share in the company. Sequoia Capital was already the VC firm for such powerhouses as Apple and 3Com. Having financed Apple, Valentine foresaw the importance of connectivity. With his commitment and wallet in place, Valentine became the de facto management that Cisco needed to effectively battle the growing number of networking companies.

Without lawyers or much time-consuming reflection, Len and Sandy signed an agreement with Valentine that granted them 30 percent of the company's stock with a 4-year vesting agreement. In return, the VC firm would provide financing, recruit management and salespeople, and create an operations process, "none of which," Don Valentine stated, "existed in the company when we arrived." Len, uninterested in any of the managerial processes, assumed the role of chief scientist, and Sandy became vice president of customer services.

Valentine's timing was impeccable. The networking industry was, as its name implies, extending and expanding posthaste. The year was a landmark in Internet history: In 1987, Congress made a commercial Internet possible, a prospect that would propel network demand into overdrive. In tandem with this event, Cisco considered how it would take the Internet from the closed system of the military and National Science Foundation elite and make it available to the rank and file. More important to the company's financial success was the need for corporations to find solutions for connecting computer networks that, without the translation of a router, could not connect to other parts of their businesses.

The demand for routers increased dramatically by the late 1980s. By that time, personal computers (PCs) were rampant in organizations worldwide, and the corporate market was ripe for networking. Companies became interested in connecting their employees to one another, as well as their larger computer systems. Reliably connecting various incarnations of computer systems across distances—from old to new mainframes and minicomputers, both Apples and PCs—became paramount to the management of large corporations.

The corporate world, by virtue of its urgent and large-scale demand, played a major role in making the router commercially viable. In an interview for this book, Valentine admitted, "[Cisco's] one of those rare companies that was started at a moment in time where the problem was so vital that customers would pay in advance." Sequoia's decision to invest in Len and Sandy's networking business was providential. Cisco was an antidote to chaos. As Valentine recognized in retrospect, "Apple in 1977 solved no problem. It had to create the application. Yahoo! in 1997 had to create a business model. But Cisco in 1987 filled a desperate need. Customers were tearing the hinges off the door to get the products. I never met a company that entered the market in such a timely way with no competition." Because the marketplace was ripe for embracing the router technology and was fueled by the PC industry, Cisco never used Sequoia's $2.5 million in 1987—or ever (although it did give the company more legitimacy and leverage). Because it didn't have the development costs or long receivables, the cash quickly flowed in and pooled in Cisco's coffers.

DON VALENTINE'S SEQUOIA CAPITAL

Ever since he founded Sequoia Capital in 1972, Don Valentine has been one the most successful venture capitalists and master builders of the technology industry of the late twentieth century. Valentine says that his success is based on his knowledge of the microprocessor industry and "being in the right place at the right time." His role in making the future happen is documented by his participation as an early investor in 3Com, Apple Computer, Atari, Oracle, Electronic Arts, Inc., and various biotech entities. When Sandy and Len pitched Cisco to him in 1986, Valentine offered $2.5 million. He also became the company's chairman of the board from 1986 to 1995. The most valued memory of his career as VC was, he gleams, the Valentine's Day (February 16, really) when Cisco went public. Then, the $2.5 million that Valentine had invested in 1987 (worth 30 percent of the company) became worth around $10 billion. Valentine added that it takes time to build up the relationships and knowledge base required to make a successful investment. He lamented, "We have bazillions of dollars and not enough successful practitioners."

■ A SEED IN SILICON VALLEY

From 1984, the year Len and Sandy founded Cisco, to 1987, when Don Valentine stepped in, the networking industry boomed. Before most of its future rivals, Cisco had a vision of a networked world where companies and even individuals would be linked via the Internet. By 1987, the year Congress opened up the ARPAnet/Internet to the world, this prophecy had begun to materialize, as the number of online hosts jacked up to more than 28,000. Cisco not only had its timing right, but its choice of location as well. Silicon Valley, which seems to emanate from the Stanford University campus, was considered a major hub.

The Valley had been sowing and reaping new technological developments at record pace. In 1983, the year before Len and Sandy founded Cisco, Scott McNealy, Vinod Khosla, Bill Joy, and Andy Bechtolsheim took SUN commercial (or, as Stanford University contends, hijacked it) to sell the workstations under the name Sun Microsystems. Sun would grow to become a $10 billion market leader along with Microsoft and Cisco. In 1985, SynOptics (a spin-off from Xerox PARC, like 3Com) pioneered the technology that resulted in the important 10BaseT connection-wiring standard for the Ethernet. The following year, Mitsui Comtek, an outpost of Mitsui & Co. of Japan, makers of the first laptop computer, became a Silicon Valley neighbor. The 1986 World Exposition was the first world's fair to be, thanks to the Internet, simultaneously witnessed worldwide. By 1987, the number of Sun workstation users had increased so much that Sun Microsystems founded Workstation Technologies in order to provide support. In 1987, Cisco issued its first coffee mug.

Cisco wasn't the only company that tried to become the IBM of internetworking. The entire industry began to consolidate. Bridge and 3Com, also in the networking business, were its predominant competitors. In 1987, 3Com acquired Bridge. 3Com was dominant in the LAN market, and Bridge, which had gone public in 1985, built equipment that connected terminals to host mainframes. William Carrico was made president of the combined company. Although the merger seemed sensible, Bob Metcalfe, 3Com founder, described it to me as horrible. "3Com was two or three times bigger than Bridge at that time, but we treated it as a merger of equals, which was stupid. We ended up with two heads of sales, two heads of France, two heads of Germany, two heads of marketing, two heads of engineering, and they spent the next couple of years trying to kill each other." On top of that, Metcalfe and the board discovered that, in their opinion, Carrico was "a meddling small-company kind of guy who doesn't know how to manage managers of managers of managers." Unsurprisingly, Carrico left soon after, with his wife Judy Estrin, who later became Cisco's chief technology officer and senior vice president, in tow. Whatever chance Bridge Networks or 3Com had of beating Cisco in the networking market was obliterated by the bloody merger.

Although Cisco and its Silicon Valley high-tech peers like Sun Microsystems were the strongest and most influential players in the early internetworking industry, they weren't the only innovators. Back at MIT, a stronghold of computing innovation in the 1960s and 1970s, computer scientists had made similar inventions and started their own companies. A little-mentioned formative counterpart to Cisco was the start-up Proteon Associates, founded by MIT alumnus Howard Salwen, known as the father of token-ring technology. Sun Microsystems' main competitor was Apollo, which had in fact developed similar workstations earlier. But the West Coast's emphasis on open standards and a cutthroat, do-or-die business mentality quickly demolished the East Coast competition without notable bloodshed. Cisco would enter its next stage of growth as an unhampered victor.

Chapter

The Morgridge Years
(1988–1995)

■ TURF WARS ■ IPO (INVENTORS PUSHED OUT)
■ MORGRIDGE'S MIRTH ■ AT THE HELM OF A TIGHT SHIP
■ ESTABLISHING CUSTOMER RELATIONSHIPS
■ LESSONS FROM THE PAST FOR SUCCESS IN THE FUTURE
■ CRESCENDO, THEN BOOM ■ MANAGING INFORMATION

There is a saying in Silicon Valley: You need to be more careful when selecting your venture capitalist than you are in selecting your spouse. The reason: You'll end up spending more time with the VC. If the entrepreneurs and the money people are not compatible, there's bound to be trouble.

Sandy Lerner and Len Bosack learned that lesson the hard way. After they signed the contracts with Sequoia Capital, Don Valentine exercised his right to choose the executive management team. Sandy was vice president of customer service and Len was chief technology officer. Valentine did not touch their positions, but began to replace other members of the management team with people he could trust to run a professional corporation. As more and more people were replaced with employees that

Valentine brought in, animosity grew between himself and the founders, particularly the outspoken Sandy. Her theory was that Valentine, by decimating the original culture, was systematically pushing her and her husband out.

■ TURF WARS

Most significant, Valentine decided to find a new president and chief executive officer (CEO). He wanted someone who was an industry veteran, a proven leader, a fiscal conservative, and a grown-up presence. Ironically, the best place to find such executives is often at a company that is failing. Companies in trouble shed their best executives first. In what was going to become a major theme at Cisco, Valentine found an executive who had just achieved what is often considered a badge of honor in risk-loving Silicon Valley: living through a failure.

Around mid-1988, John P. Morgridge, president of Grid Systems, the then-ailing portable computer manufacturer, was seeking another job. "It was dreadful," Morgridge stressed to Silicon Valley journalist Karen Southwick. "Companies have personalities. Have you ever met someone for whom, no matter how they live, life is always trouble? That was Grid. Every day I'd come home and my wife would say, 'What happened today?' And something had always happened. A supplier crapped out. The government put a 100 percent duty on flat plasma screens. It was endless." His headhunter put him in touch with Valentine.

Tandy purchased Grid around the time Morgridge was debating whether to accept Valentine's offer. Considering the fact that top executives of an acquired company are often kicked out by the management of the acquiring company, you would think Morgridge would have jumped at the chance. But he didn't want to make the same mistake twice, so he decided to research Cisco. "I got a list of customers," admitted Morgridge. "It wasn't a long list: a dozen names. I called them all and got through to eight. I asked three questions: Are you currently using the Cisco product? Do you like it? And are you going to buy more? All eight answered yes to all three questions." So Morgridge took the job. "It seemed like a logical decision."

The 54-year-old executive made a wise choice. When he accepted the offer, he was granted Cisco stock options worth about 6 percent of the company. Valentine may have guessed that he was about to cash in by investing in a networking start-up. The use of personal computers at corporations was beginning to explode. That meant more computer networks and a growing need to make sure the different networks would be able to talk to each other. Cisco, at the time, was producing router technology that was to become the de facto standard.

When Valentine recruited him, Morgridge's experience included the two-year position as president and chief operating officer at Grid Systems, a marketing vice president position at Stratus Computers, and many years as a salesman at Honeywell. None of these companies has survived as a major player today. Before Honeywell, Morgridge's core of personal discipline was cultivated by the three years he served in the Air Force after graduating from the University of Wisconsin's graduate school of business.

Morgridge was hired by Valentine and sided with the VC when it came to dealing with the founders. He was entering a business with a very close-knit culture engendered by the founders—a "family" that was somewhat hostile to the imposed management. What made matters worse was that Valentine didn't even consult with the founders before hiring the new president.

Morgridge, as the new boss, found himself sparring with the company's founders every step of the way. Cisco was becoming a real corporation, and Sandy in particular was not the corporate type. Sandy had always been a self-proclaimed rebel and iconoclast. Her aunts raised her after her parents divorced when she was 4. She refused to pledge allegiance in grade school, got in trouble with the police for protesting the Vietnam War when she was 13, graduated from high school at 16, and received her bachelor's degree in 2 years. She has maintained these character traits today. In an unprecedented issue of *Forbes* magazine, she posed nude, on a horse, for a photo—probably the first time a company executive has been pictured naked in a major U.S. business magazine.

As a first order of business, Morgridge decided that it would be advantageous to hire a company psychologist to "reconcile" all the motley personalities—he knew that the founders weren't happy with Valentine's meddling. To the shrink's credit or culpability, Sandy's resentment only grew in time. She'd come into his office every day and discharge. Passions flared on both sides. Sandy started to complain that the company was losing sight of the customers. Morgridge admitted to Southwick in an unpublished interview, "I think Sandy would have liked to have been president, but Cisco would have turned out to be a far different company."

■ IPO (INVENTORS PUSHED OUT)

By late 1989, Morgridge and Valentine and Sandy and Len agreed on just one thing: that the company should go public. George Kelly, a technology analyst at Morgan Stanley, had visited Cisco and encouraged Morgridge to follow through on the initial public offering (IPO). Kelly's research revealed that Cisco was at least two years ahead of its competitors, was developing industry standards, and already had an array of eminent clients including the U.S. Army, Boeing, Hewlett-Packard, General Electric, and Morgan Stanley. In fiscal year 1989, Cisco made $4.2 million in profits; then it raked in another $2.5 million in the first quarter of fiscal year 1990. The math looked good.

On February 16, its first day of trading, Cisco stock opened at $18 a share and closed at around $22.50. Any individual with the savvy to invest $1,000 in Cisco and Morgridge at the IPO would have scored over $100,000 in 1999. But most buyers of Cisco stock in 1990 were institutions. George Kelly of Morgan Stanley became known on Wall Street as "Mr. Cisco" for his unceasing "buy" recommendation for Cisco stock.

Six months after the IPO, a cataclysm occurred. The seven Cisco VPs in place at the time had banded together in mutual loathing for Sandy and presented their case to Morgridge. They said that they found her intolerable to work with. She would often barge into their offices, shouting about something that Cisco was doing wrong. Further, she would refuse to take no for an answer when a customer needed something, no matter how impossible the request. Morgridge had tried to construct a management team that could work together in an atmosphere of trust, but Sandy didn't trust the other VPs and the VPs didn't trust her. The VPs told Morgridge that they had agreed to a pact: Either Sandy Lerner would go, or all seven of them would quit. After presenting their case to Morgridge, they trundled over to Don Valentine's office with the same threat. Never a huge fan of Sandy's people skills, Valentine conceded, and Sandy was asked to go.

To make matters worse, as Sandy realized in retrospect, the original contract she and Len had signed with Don Valentine didn't offer her much protection. The agreement they signed contained no employment contract. It was, as Len described later to reporters of the PBS show *Nerds 2.0,* a pact to "indentured servitude" in which Valentine would have the right to purchase back Len and Sandy's shares if they didn't do as he asked. Luckily, it never came to that.

On August 28, 1990, Sandy was shown the door. Len quit as a member of the board, and soon thereafter quit altogether. In December, they jointly decided to sell their two-thirds stake in Cisco for about $170 million. Valentine chided them later, stating that if they had decided to "suffer their outrage with more financial wisdom," and kept on as investors, they would be far richer. The loss didn't visibly faze Sandy, who merely retorted to Valentine that she didn't want her money in the hands of people she didn't like. (Incidentally, the sudden surplus of Cisco stock was a boon for Wall Street. Those in the know eagerly snapped up the shares.)

On Wall Street, Cisco stock started out as a prudent buy and quickly became a Wall Street darling. Some of this was due to the company's escalating sales and the excellent reputation it had gained, but part of it was due to a clever strategy by Cisco's chief financial officer, John Bolger. Then, as today (unless you're a *dot-com* company), if you really want to charm those clever boys on the Street, you have to have a few tricks for keeping expectations low and results high, yet without attracting the attention of the Securities and Exchange Commission. Bolger was no slouch. Corporate sales normally follow a formation shaped somewhat like a hockey stick: Sales are flat in the first two months of a quarter, then spike up in the last month of the quarter. Under Bolger's direction, Cisco scheduled its backlog to reverse the pattern, making most of its sales in the beginning of each quarter, then tapering at the end. Customers didn't appreciate the backlogs that would occur, but Cisco gained significant credibility on the Street when it easily met its targets.

Morgan Stanley's George Kelly, of course, remained optimistic about Cisco. So did most other Wall Street analysts. Mary Henry of Goldman Sachs was the most critical, and Bolger encouraged her pessimism in order to keep public expectations in line. Bolger tried, without actually lying, to keep all the analysts from being too enthusiastic (or accurate) in their expectations for Cisco. He called it "managing the consensus."

LIFE AFTER CISCO

Despite everything, no one can say the company's founders fared badly from their experience. They are still active in business and in social life. They remain friends today, although they divorced soon before leaving Cisco because, as Sandy proclaimed, they had nothing to talk about. It was also the stress, the work, the low pay, and the company, Sandy said later, that did them in. Seventy percent of the money they made from the Cisco stock remains split between two charitable funds: a joint fund, the Leonard X. Bosack and Bette M. Kruger Charitable Foundation (named after Len's father and Sandy's mother), and Ampersand Capital, an umbrella charitable trust that provides funding for everything from aiding lost pets to the search for extraterrestrial life.

With the rest of his half, Len moved to Redmond, Washington. When he jumped the Cisco ship for his new venture, XKL, he brought some of the original Cisco founders with him. XKL produces server-class computing and networking equipment, but has certainly not enjoyed Cisco-class success.

Sandy, meanwhile, gained notoriety by posing naked on a horse for an issue of *Forbes* magazine that described Cisco's lustrous past. She occupies her time jousting Renaissance-style, riding her horses, mixing music on her Macintosh, occasionally dating, and planning new ventures. She traveled after leaving Cisco, and in 1992 she purchased Chawton House, a 50-room, 22,000-square-foot mansion on 275 acres of farmland in Chawton, England, that used to belong to Jane Austen's brother. Her intent is to convert the house into a Jane Austen study center for early English women's literature—after its nineteenth-century roof is restored, its plumbing and electrical

(continued)

LIFE AFTER CISCO
(Continued)

---

systems are replaced, and its interior is renovated. Lerner became as notorious with the British press as she had been within Silicon Valley circles, as locals shuddered at the idea of a Californian owning such a heritage. Articles speculating on Sandy's true plans for Chawton House included the possibilities that she would turn it into a lesbian commune, open another Euro-Disney park, or make it into a base for a virtual reality missile-guidance program. Sandy lives there and on her 800-acre farm in Loudoin County, Virginia.

Notorious for her energy, Sandy also founded the cosmetics start-up company Urban Decay in 1995. Under the tagline "Does pink make you puke?" UD's line of nail polishes and lipsticks come in an array of volatile colors with suggestive names like bruise, frostbite, gash, toxin, asphyxia, and oil slick. Dennis Rodman started sporting UD products, as did Drew Barrymore, Sean Lennon, the cast of *Melrose Place,* and a Siamese twin in the 1999 movie *Twin Falls Idaho.*

■ MORGRIDGE'S MIRTH

John Morgridge set the tone for the Cisco culture that exists to this day. He continued Cisco's tradition of tight-fistedness, customer focus, risk taking, and open doors. Morgridge ran the company on trust and hard-nosed spirit.

Among the first talent attracted to Cisco was Barbara Beck, Cisco's forty-fifth employee and Morgridge's first hire back in 1989. In her decade-long tenure at the company, Beck was one of the few to have witnessed Morgridge's long-term contouring of the corporate culture. "Sometimes Morgridge was a challenge to follow because he always said exactly what was on his mind," she told reporter Southwick tactfully. One of her favorite Morgridge stories is about the time when one employee griped to the CEO about a drop in the value of Cisco stock. His stock options were now worth less than those of newer employees. The impetuous Morgridge casually replied, "You can always quit and see if we rehire you."

"John also has a personal ingredient I consider very important," admitted Don Valentine, "the ability to be outrageous." Morgridge was chummy with his staff. In board meetings, Morgridge would call up all the people who were recently married and publicly rail them, "What did you do last night?" Described as blunt, yet friendly, undiplomatic, and a riot by the people working under him, Morgridge was just as offhand with his peers. In negotiations with other CEOs, Morgridge would blurt out, "Who's going to get rich out of this one?" But he is also direct, clear, and incisive when it comes to difficult questions such as whether a promise is going to materialize or why an undesirable event occurred.

■ AT THE HELM OF A TIGHT SHIP

In those heady years following the IPO and the booting of the founders, Morgridge honed the most important technique an entrepreneur needs to know: running a tight ship. His years at Honeywell had taught him enough about grand schemes and ambitious goals that never materialize. Cisco never had a five-year plan in the Morgridge years. "At Cisco we build a one-year plan with 80 to 90 percent assurance we'll meet or exceed our goals, so it's not a stretch," said Morgridge. "Then we modify the plan, because we're conservative." Not only does this help morale, but it keeps the goals in focus.

Morgridge was admittedly a small-company executive; his management style was tailored to that environment. He made sure all decisions were made directly under him by establishing a strong central team. His focused, close-knit management team at the center controlled all aspects of the company. He established the central divisions of manufacturing, customer support, finance, human resources, information technology, sales, product marketing, and research and development. All except the last two, which would later be decentralized across product lines, remain Cisco's enduring organizational core.

Morgridge had another start-up executive trait: stinginess with the company's money. Like Sandy, Morgridge never spent the $2.5 million from Sequoia. He has followed the tradition of Sandy and Len, who, by legend, built the company on savings and credit-card debt. "John is the only president we've ever financed who is cheaper than I am," boasted Don Valentine. "And I am very cheap. One of the things I was warned about when we were doing reference checks on him a long time ago was that when you have dinner with him, don't let him choose the wine. I've always carefully heeded that advice." A Milwaukee native born in the Depression era who maintained that mindset throughout his leadership, Morgridge's scrimping was his way of ensuring that his company would be prosperous.

However, Morgridge would spend big bucks for things that he felt were crucial to the company's success. In 1992, as part of Morgridge's mission to centralize—and to remain centralized despite the temptation to go forth and multiply—he lobbied the board of directors to purchase 50 acres of real estate in nearby North San Jose. The board was at first dubious, claiming that Morgridge wanted to acquire an awful lot of real estate. Nevertheless, the CEO prevailed. For the next two years, as the new headquarters were being constructed, Cisco was a growing adolescent squeezed into the same 120,000-square-foot Menlo Park space that the founders had purchased when Cisco employed only 10 people. By 1992, Cisco had over 800 employees. A few of them, however, happened to be in Japan, where Cisco opened its first subsidiary—Nihon Cisco—that year. Morgridge's purchase of the new headquarters was a significant act of trust in Cisco's future.

Himself at the bottom of the salary lists of CEOs, Morgridge would lecture his executives on indulgences such as flying first class on business trips. In a directors' meeting, Morgridge would set up all the chairs in the configuration of coach versus business class. In good-natured satire, he would instruct the executives to "go virtual first class," and steal a mask and slippers from the first-class seats on the way to coach. To him, business isn't about luxury; it's about attitude. He really doesn't like to see executives believe that they deserve better than everyone else. "Someone flies first class, no one else does; he gets a suite, no one else does. You can run the company that way, but don't expect employees to be excited about it." Morgridge himself would fly on senior discount coupons and get upgrades only when he attained enough frequent flyer miles. It was this philosophy that helped to strengthen the culture of community at Cisco.

Cisco is at least egalitarian in its stinginess: All employees were (and remain) lower paid on average than those of comparable companies in the industry. Paltry paychecks, however, are leveraged by bonuses and stock options higher than the industry standard. Cisco adopted the Silicon Valley perspective of using stock to keep employees invested in the success of the entire company. Lousy pay in exchange for rich stock options and generous bonuses for great corporate performance are standard operating procedure in Silicon Valley today. But Morgridge tried to cut back on one perk that is also a Valley tradition: free beverages.

Since the Lerner and Bosack days, Cisco had provided soft drinks to its employees. A few years into Morgridge's term, the frugal CEO tried to reduce the variety from around 50 flavors to 24. The staff was furious. Cisco's electronic culture thrived on the dispute. Renegade e-mails spread throughout the company with gripes about "second-class citizenship" and the "right to Snapple." Morgridge grimly admitted that it shut the place down. (Not really!) Needless to say, the 24-flavor plan lasted only about 1 week. If nothing else, Cisco was and is as egalitarian as capitalism gets. With enough critical mass behind it, the soda-pop issue was resolved in favor of the people. Another "take home" for Morgridge from the pop experience was never to offer employees anything they wouldn't relinquish without a fight or a decrease in morale. So he didn't offer any more perks or promises that he couldn't consistently provide.

■ ESTABLISHING CUSTOMER RELATIONSHIPS

Customer commitment remains crucial to Cisco's core culture. Morgridge himself attributes Cisco's extraordinary growth in its adolescent and adult years to strong customer relations—the backbone of most industry giants. Under Morgridge, Cisco primarily sold routers directly to large corporations. By assessing not only the market, but the players and, moreover, the captains, Cisco maneuvered itself into the boardrooms of the individuals with the deepest pockets. Morgridge sold Cisco products not to technical staff but to upper management. This strategy quickly caused Cisco to become well known among the elite and well-funded of the technology world, yet the company remained largely unfamiliar among medium- and small-business owners—and among the public at large. "The joke around here," quipped one Cisco employee, "is that we're the most important company that no one's ever heard of."

Not much was written about Cisco in the media in the early 1990s, another good reason why few knew Morgridge's name or what, exactly, Cisco manufactured and sold. But Cisco's targeted clientele was online—and Cisco gained a reputation among potential customers by being a significant Internet presence when the Net was just being introduced to general users. Morgridge made it Cisco's priority to develop an innovative use of technology for customer support. (Ironically, this had been Sandy Lerner's focus as well.)

Douglas Allred, vice president for customer advocacy (who replaced Sandy Lerner), and Mark Tonneson, Cisco's director of customer advocacy, fortified the new networking business by identifying emerging markets for routers. They discovered that Cisco's customers used their routers in unexpected ways and through extensive research learned what potential customers expected their networks to do. Cisco then provided those companies with the necessary technology, service, and flexibility. Cisco's immeasurable popularity among its growing customer base can be credited to four primary approaches: Listen to the customer, hire technical salespeople, use the Internet, and help customers help themselves.

➤ Listen to the Customers

Because networking is intrinsically about compatibility and communication, Cisco is tied to its customers both through its products and its philosophy. Morgridge was really hot on listening to customers and giving them what they wanted. He gave them fixes, tweaks, improvements, complaints, demands, and, in general, opportunities for future sales.

Under Morgridge's tenure, Cisco emphasized the role its customers played in developing increasingly advanced products and using technology to meet growing customer demands. In a company that had no single, fastidious vision, customer input had an enormous effect on Cisco's actions. Instead of *introducing* new tools to the marketplace, Cisco listened to the market and responded to its explicit demands. "We had the advantage of selling to a peer group," Morgridge notes, "and we responded to their requirements." It was a sweet spot to be in, as he put it, one that put Cisco in a position to grow with its customers as an actualized lifeline. In fact, Cisco's attachment to its customers eventually led it to the acquisition strategy central to its mind-boggling success. Cisco's vision of what the future of computing would look like and its relentless pursuit of creating and filling the market's needs are among its hallmarks as a company.

➤ Hire Technical Salespeople

Cisco didn't even bother to advertise its routers until 1992, when it already had more than $300 million in annual revenues. Until then, it succeeded by word of mouth and contacts over the Internet. In the beginning, it was Cisco's superlative technical sales force that made the company distinctive. The hotshot engineers who pioneered the router protocols would also service the customers. The clients would call the engineers directly, and they'd talk about the technology and how it could be customized according to the customer's needs. At first, this use of the engineers' time wasn't a big problem; the customers were savvy enough that their questions led directly to product improvements. As sales grew, however, Cisco's commitment to customer service began to clash with the need to protect the engineers from time-consuming support calls. Cisco found the answer in the very open community it was helping to grow—the Internet.

➤ Use the Internet

From its conception in 1984, the Internet was the foundation for Cisco's customer relations and sales strategies. Len and Sandy sold their garage-made routers to colleagues over the first filaments of the Web. The Cisco site had grown in response to the pervasiveness of the Web. In 1989, Allred implemented a customer support site, where customers could download software and software upgrades to complement the software packages the company sent out on floppy disk or CD-ROM. In 1990, the site featured a bug-report database—a valuable addition that enabled customers and software developers to prevent potential infestations. With the bug database, customers could find out whether their problem was unique and, if not, how other customers solved it.

By 1993, the beginning of Cisco's growth spurt, Allred installed an Internet-based system for their large multinational enterprise customers. These customers had the privilege of posting problems and questions. After fruitlessly searching the bug-report database, for example, a customer could post a problem on the site for the Cisco tech staff to tackle. Soon after the posting capability was implemented, customers began responding to other customers' questions. A single problem would often prompt several suggestions, solutions, and workarounds. Cisco installed a trigger function that would send out an e-mail alerting the posting customer to check out the database if another customer responded to a query. Soon thereafter, Cisco opened up the system to its smaller customers, as well. Cisco customers worldwide began posting messages and e-mailing other Cisco customers on the Cisco site. Cisco.com became one of the first online corporate communities.

Although Cisco grew exponentially in the years thereafter, its support call center didn't. The posting feature proved itself a boon to engineers, who could focus on the difficult calls filtered out by the site. If it weren't for the site, Doug Allred once determined, Cisco would have had to hire up to 10,000 engineers to keep up with Cisco's growth.

➤ Help Customers Help Themselves

The Internet is, in effect, Cisco's research and development lab, as well as its salesroom and customer support desk. The site and database at cisco.com became the conduit for sales and customer support. In 1994, cisco.com was christened "The Cisco Connection Online." Since Cisco first introduced online order status, over 70 percent of all nontechnical support inquiries have shifted from call centers to the Web. Soon after introducing online ordering, Cisco posted its price lists on the site with worldwide currency conversions. Customers—as well as dealers and distributors—could then just help themselves to the information.

Cisco's next—and more difficult—step toward making itself self-service was to install an online configuration system. When Cisco first introduced online ordering, customers could place orders for equipment combinations that didn't make sense—the equivalent, for example, of ordering a convertible car with a roof rack. Mark Tonneson therefore purchased a new configuration system from Calico—a software system that customers could use to simulate a network using Cisco equipment in order to see if all the components ordered were compatible. A customer could therefore spend hours alone on the Net testing different combinations, again freeing the customer service personnel to handle specific questions and cases.

Cisco's Web site grew technologically and demographically in the years following Morgridge's appointment as CEO. But Allred and Tonneson's work laid the foundation for what would later be one of the best Web sites on the Net.

■ LESSONS FROM THE PAST FOR SUCCESS IN THE FUTURE

In 1993, Cisco's market capitalization hit $714 million. To make Cisco a multibillion-dollar company in the mid-1990s and beyond, Morgridge required a business plan beyond his initial strategies to stay centralized, be frugal, remain true to the customer, and foster community. So Morgridge and his cadre—John Chambers, senior vice president of world operations, and Ed Kozel, the chief technology officer—got down to work. The primary goal for Cisco was to move beyond the router market. In fact, customers such as Boeing and Ford were showing interest in emerging alternative networking technologies, like switching. This would be an important test. Diversification is the point at which most fledgling companies begin to fail. To create the points of the business plan, the Cisco team decided to adopt the corporate philosophies of companies that were successful at providing a wide array of related products.

Cisco needed to expand like wildfire because the rise of the Internet was upon the United States and the rest of the world. This global network precipitated an explosion in all networks, making companies want and need more technology than simply routers. Future markets for Cisco included security software to allow companies to share information safely, firewalls to keep out snoops and viruses, and modems to connect individual PCs to the sprawling Internet through phone lines. Advances in the underlying networks, like Fast Ethernet and Asynchronous Transfer Mode (ATM), were similarly driving the networking boom. New companies were sprouting up everywhere to enter the fray, and all threatened to beat Cisco at the networking game.

The companies that the team studied were General Electric, IBM, and Hewlett-Packard. Although Cisco was, at the time, little more than a router provider, Morgridge and the others realized that the external pressure to move beyond routers was an opportunity for Cisco to expand its range of solutions and set standards for an array of networking technologies. Other companies, faced with the same problem, became religious about their technology and were unwilling to embrace change.

For guidance on how to find success in all market segments, Cisco looked to General Electric. GE's CEO Jack Welch had a simple philosophy that effectively guided the company: With every product, be number one or number two, or don't compete at all.

The Cisco team analyzed IBM to learn what worked in the computing industry. Having spent six years of his career in sales at IBM, Chambers knew that Big Blue dominated computing in the 1960s and 1970s by supplying soup-to-nuts data-processing solutions. Cisco had the opportunity to do the same in internetworking. However, IBM's corporate organization had been too rigid to allow adaptation, and IBM had suffered greatly during the 1980s. Cisco had to stay flexible as it expanded. Chambers planned to apply IBM's sales and organizational philosophies at the height of its success to Cisco. Though many, including himself, saw IBM's decay as a cautionary tale, he also deeply admired IBM's time of success.

Hewlett-Packard, also one of the first computer companies in the world, was the only strong survivor of the minicomputer era and a strong model for Cisco. HP had prospered by utterly reinventing itself as a provider of a wide range of computing solutions. Hewlett-Packard developed a flexible and dynamic corporate structure and business philosophy that took lessons from Japanese corporate culture. Central management established long-term strategies, while product teams independently developed and marketed products. Combining strategic management, tactical engineering, and consumer research, HP was able to intelligently divide the market for its products into complementary segments. Morgridge, Chambers, and Kozel carefully studied how HP managed separate divisions and different product lines while constantly adapting to a fickle market.

The three executives then sat down and devised a business plan that would officially replace the tentative one that Morgridge had put together when he first came on board in 1988. In early 1993, at the time the team sketched out their goals, Cisco had grown to 1,000 employees. Stronger direction was in order. Their business plan, in brief, consisted of four areas of focus for future development: Provide a complete solution for businesses, make acquisitions a structured process, define the industrywide networking software protocols, and form the right strategic alliances.

➤ Provide a Complete Solution for Businesses

The rise of the Internet and personal computing reshaped Cisco's universe. No longer was it a matter of building routers that would allow one network to talk to another. Suddenly the world was being tied together by one giant, interconnected web of high-speed networks that required much more than simply routers to keep humming. The team wanted Cisco to move from a simple horizontal monopoly in routers to the vertical monopoly of providing the Internet's backbone, emulating IBM's success in computing. They recognized that Cisco's 80 percent router monopoly would mean little when companies moved to new technologies. Only through a constant stream of acquisitions would Cisco be able to own, develop, and market a growing array of networking products and standards.

➤ Make Acquisitions a Structured Process

The question was, who would quickly expand into these new businesses? Silicon Valley was a fertile ground for start-ups. Engineers were furiously creating new equipment for the Internet and building companies around their inventions. Excited by the potential of the Internet, venture capitalists were happy to fund these start-ups by the dozens. The team decided the only way to keep up was to embark on a risky strategy of acquisitions.

Technology acquisitions are notoriously difficult to pull off. They may increase the number of products a company sells, but those products are not necessarily perfectly complementary and may not be compatible. Corporate management styles clash, and employees are embittered when colleagues are fired. Building a company through acquisitions is just as likely to create a Frankenstein's monster with a mercifully short lifespan as a new corporate behemoth.

Realizing that acquisitions would be the only way to acquire the technologies needed to dominate the market, the team had to ensure that their purchasing choices would benefit the company. They needed to be successful at a rate much higher than the market average. Other companies often had terrible experiences with acquisitions and mergers. A successful, market-leading company would merge and six months later would be in terrible shape. Another company would spend months determining the best company to acquire and not spend any time or resources on properly integrating the acquisition.

➤ Define the Industrywide Networking Software Protocols

Cisco began with routers that allowed networks using different protocols to communicate. Its equipment and software defined the open protocols that allowed the Internet to grow. Its engineers worked in the networking community to write up the papers that detailed the protocols. Morgridge, Chambers, and Kozel made it an official strategy to keep turning out better and more complex technology.

➤ Form the Right Strategic Alliances

The team realized that partnerships with other companies were not only desirable but inevitable, if Cisco were to maintain its technology lead across the board. They knew that intelligent alliances were the best method of managing competitors, getting access to new technology, and gaining entry into new markets. Their strongest influence came from negative examples like the alliance between 3Com and Microsoft in the late 1980s. Microsoft hooked up with 3Com to catch up in the networking business. In an effort to usurp Novell, the number-one network software provider of the time, the two companies decided to split up the duties: 3Com would concentrate on hardware, Microsoft on software. But everything went awry. Microsoft was in the process of disassociating itself from its partnership with IBM, which threw 3Com's expectations into disarray. When the dust cleared, 3Com had signed a deal to resell Microsoft's networking product, which was being made by 3Com—a terrible deal that was one of the deciding factors in the ouster of 3Com's founder, Bob Metcalfe.

Morgridge, Chambers, and Kozel knew that they, in contrast, would have to form alliances and partnerships that would be fair, equitable, and well thought out. Cisco became famous for forming intelligent alliances with competitors. Among Cisco's partners in the future would be its potential competitors Wellfleet, Cabletron, Synoptics, Bay Networks, AT&T, and IBM.

■ CRESCENDO, THEN BOOM

Cisco had been in negotiations with Boeing for a stout $10 million router order. Although Boeing had considered a bulk purchase of expensive Cisco routers, it was inclined to opt for the low-cost, simpler products produced by Cisco's competitor, Crescendo Communications. Crescendo, another Sequoia Capital investment, was one of the companies that had come out with an alternative networking technology based on *switches*—devices that increasingly competed with Cisco's routers.

Networking switches were the result of recent technological advances that allowed hardware to do work that could previously be done only by software running on a more expensive box. With these switches, companies could build large Ethernet LANs that were robust, fast, and inexpensive, rather than building collections of smaller LANs using hubs connected by Cisco routers. In short, switches made better, faster hubs.

In the midst of the discussions with Senior Vice President of Worldwide Operations John Chambers, the deal makers at Boeing indicated that Cisco would not get the contract unless it cooperated with—or coopted—Crescendo. Around the same time, in 1993, Ford Motor Company had told Morgridge and Chambers that it was going to opt for the newfangled switches instead of Cisco routers—a blow that likewise incited the Cisco executives to consider either partnering with or acquiring Crescendo.

The team, remembering a regretted loss from the early 1990s when they had rejected the opportunity to purchase Vitalink, a company that produced an alternative networking technology called bridging, decided that they didn't want to miss the boat again. The acquisition would enhance Cisco's product line dramatically. The business plan, after all, included the systematic acquisition of smaller networking companies, innovative entities that fueled new markets and the Cisco engine itself.

Morgridge, Chambers, and Kozel went to the board of directors for approval to acquire Crescendo for $90 million. Before the presentation, the three men were understandably nervous. Historical precedent showed that high-tech mergers didn't work. But the trio believed they had determined why it was essential for Cisco to diversify through acquisition, and the board believed their presentation. The negotiations could continue unobstructed.

In what was to become another recurring pattern at Cisco, the executives brokered a deal that made them look like naïve tourists being taken for a ride in a private taxi in Brooklyn. Wall Street couldn't believe that Cisco would spend $97 million on a company with $10 million in annual revenues. Did these guys really know what they were doing? The deal between Morgridge and Mario Mazzola, CEO of Crescendo, was peacefully brokered; the acquisition cost Cisco $97 million. When the acquisition was announced, industry analysts shook their heads. Cisco's stock took a dip for the first time. One Wall Street analyst, Paul Johnson of First Boston, perceived the acquisition as

THE MARIO RULE

Crescendo's CEO was concerned about how his employees would be treated after moving to Cisco. Usually, the management of an acquired company is fired. And whenever there is overlap—two accounting departments, for example—it's the staff from the acquired company that gets the axe.

One enduring principle born of the Crescendo acquisition is the *Mario rule,* named in honor of Sicilian-born Senior Vice President Mario Mazzola, the former CEO of Crescendo. The Mario rule stipulates that before any employee of a newly acquired company is terminated, both CEOs must give their consent. The message Cisco would like to send to new employees is that Cisco cares for their well-being in a way that most corporate acquisitors don't.

a desperate move on Cisco's part and downgraded its stock. Other analysts followed, considering the networking marketplace to be fickle. But by July, at the end of fiscal 1994, Cisco was bringing in over $1 billion in annual revenues and had expanded to 2,262 employees. By 1996, the Crescendo team alone produced more than $500 million in annual revenue.

■ MANAGING INFORMATION

The acquisition of Crescendo placed a burden on Cisco's undeveloped information technology (IT) division. Crescendo's computer systems and business processes had to be integrated into Cisco's. In stepped Chief Information Officer Peter Solvik, who had witnessed the Crescendo deal at the beginning of his Cisco career in 1993 and was determined to make Crescendo the first of many acquisition successes. But when he took a look at the information technology he had inherited, Solvik quickly realized that his department was woefully unprepared to meet the expectations that Morgridge, Chambers, and Kozel had laid out in their business plan.

Solvik took several major steps to allow budgetary decisions to be made by functional areas but still have the IT organization report along centralized channels. The first thing he did at Cisco was to decentralize the central applications development budget. Solvik liberated IT from the constraints of central management, which regarded his department as a necessary evil and tried to minimize its expenses. He returned control of the business functions' IT budgets to the individual divisions, announcing that IT would carry out the projects that the divisions chose to fund. This made a majority of the IT budget client-funded. For example, a manufacturing executive would decide how much money to spend on IT to reach certain productivity goals, but Solvik and his people would determine how to deliver on the executive's needs, keeping in mind Cisco's corporate strategy.

Once the administrative details were resolved, Solvik hurled himself into resolving the problems regarding the technology itself. Modern companies need to be run by computer. Rather than relying on paper invoices and telephone conversations, big corporations need to store all the information in databases that offer up the necessary information instantly. Cisco's information systems were a transaction-processing Unix-based software package with different screens for financial, manufacturing, and order/entry data. While this system was certainly much more efficient than its paper equivalents, it couldn't do much more than they could. In fact, wading through Cisco's transaction-processing software was a daunting task.

To complicate matters, Solvik had to execute an IT strategy that would be flexible enough to fulfill the needs of Cisco's new independently acting business units. He expected the separate departments to make decisions on upgrades to the package, but to use common databases and architecture. But Solvik feared the move to a complex, integrated system that would automate the processes of taking orders, buying equipment, ordering new parts for the factory, producing the right number and types of products for customers, and so on. The complicated software programs that run these processes are called enterprise resource planning (ERP) programs. He knew that implementing an ERP system had the potential to become a megaproject that could swallow the entire company from the inside.

Randy Pond, a manufacturing engineer, also knew the department was in trouble. One of his responsibilities was to constantly band-aid the existing system. Pond wanted the system replaced. The problem, Pond realized, was that IT would have to go to the board and demand $5 million or $6 million to buy a package that, in addition to its grandiose expense, it would take over a year to install. Even worse, it would disrupt the company in the process.

Solvik saw his world dying in dribs and drabs. He soon found that the incremental upgrades were insufficient to handle booming Cisco. The package just could not scale with Cisco's 80 percent annual growth. His engineers, unable to deal with the many layers of unorganized code on top of the core database, referred to the system as "too much spaghetti." The internal network locked up ever more frequently. Each recovery was more difficult than the last, as unfixed problems in the sales software built up like a tarry residue. In January 1994, not long after the Crescendo integration, the big crash came. Because the system wasn't properly extensible, a hole had been punched through the "spaghetti" to allow direct access to the core database. A method exploiting the hole malfunctioned, and Cisco's information center was corrupted. Cisco shut down for two days.

It was time to do the ERP renovation. Solvik got together with a number of the managers, including Pond, and announced a call to arms. Senior Vice President of Manufacturing Carl Redfield (who had come from Digital) took action. "Okay, let's get on with this," he told the team of managers. His plan was to start from the manufacturing perspective and get the other groups in the company interested in replacing all the existing software applications. Redfield knew from his experience at Digital that the project needed to be done fast and all at once to prevent such an endeavor from becoming a monster.

A team headed by Redfield, Solvik, Pond, and project manager Tom Herbert got under way. They brought in people essential to all functions of Cisco, to the chagrin of those people's bosses. To choose the software vendor, the team of 20 asked successful corporations, accounting firms, and research firms such as the Gartner Group for advice. Within two days there were five candidates. A week later, after scrutinizing the packages and the companies—Cisco did not want to put its future in the hands of a start-up—there were two: Oracle and another major ERP vendor. The team sent out the request for proposals (RFP) for an ERP system and gave the vendors two weeks to reply. After walking through three-day software presentations, the team made its choice.

Oracle won for a number of reasons, including strength in manufacturing and long-term promises (some of which ultimately never met the contractual deadlines). Cisco went far out on a limb when it chose Oracle. At the time, Oracle had little track record building the ERP applications Cisco needed. But its greatest asset was being a Silicon Valley company like Cisco. True to his original emphasis on the centralization of location, Morgridge loved the fact that Oracle was only 20 miles away. Oracle's people were able to convince Cisco that their intelligence outweighed their inexperience. They promised Cisco the newest and the best. Because Oracle had no track record, it wanted to prove it could actually pull this project off for a customer. So in classic Silicon Valley style, it offered a really cheap price as a newcomer to the business (which appealed to Morgridge), and, in exchange, stipulated that Cisco would have to brag about the new system from Oracle once it was working.

But first the IT and manufacturing team had to do their job and get approval from the board. They realized the project needed to be scoped, completed, and go live in nine months, by January 1995, to fit with Cisco's quarterly schedule. Even with cut-rate pricing from Oracle, the price tag came to a frightening $15 million. But the company had no choice. It needed a new system.

When Solvik, Pond, and Herbert showed the proposal to Morgridge, the CEO was not amused. They went pale as he told them that careers were lost over much less money than the amount they were demanding for the ERP. Like the Cosa Nostra, Cisco would not be forgiving if the project went awry. But Morgridge did give his blessing (or sentencing) to the team to present the proposal to the board.

The team trundled into the boardroom with a stack of carefully thought out slides, their well-prepared notes, and an ace in the hole. As they walked in, the team announced that the system was down again—with impeccable timing, it had crashed that very morning. All emergencies aside, however, the price tag would still take some convincing.

Before the group turned on the projector, chairman Don Valentine spoke from the shadows in the back of the room. "How much?" he asked. Pond replied that they would get to that slide, but Valentine interrupted him. "I hate surprises," he said. "Just put the slide up right now." Pond grudgingly found the guilty figure and flashed it on the screen. Valentine sardonically gasped, "God, there better be a lot of good slides. . . ." Fortunately, there were. The board gave its okay, and Morgridge made the ERP project a companywide priority.

The IT team expanded from 20 members to 5 groups of 20. From executives down to personnel, Cisco, Oracle, and KPMG, a consultancy skilled in ERP implementation, all collaborated. During the next few months, the implementation team struggled with various challenges. They decided to keep none of the legacy systems; all information was recoded into a new central data warehouse.

The system frequently crashed at first, but by May 1995, four months overdue, all problems were ironed out and Cisco arguably had the most advanced ERP system on the planet. Its information system (IS), which Solvik moved cleanly to the Web era, has remained the envy of Fortune 500 companies and a subject of study for top-flight business schools. In the end, Pete Solvik's team was awarded a $200,000 bonus, and Randy Pond was promoted to the vice-president level in manufacturing. Though Cisco had rewarded performance with cash bonuses in the past, this amount was unprecedented. The risk Solvik and his team had taken had paid off for the individuals and, certainly, for Cisco, too, as it lurched ahead.

Little did Pete Solvik know that years later this ERP process would become one of Chambers's success story anecdotes. Cisco's IS had become a key competitive advantage. In 1997, Pete Solvik would make a presentation to the board of directors about the productivity resulting from the IS implementation. Chambers gleefully recounts how, after Solvik left the room, the toughest board member of all said, "John, not only are we very pleased with how the company has done here, but we should give this guy a raise." The moral of the story, says Chambers, is that "even the most conservative people are suddenly realizing that if you pick the right applications, it can have huge productivity advantages and also can be what separates you from your competition and perhaps not only determines your growth rate, but who survives [in this industry]."[1]

Chapter

The Inner Chambers (1977–1995)

When John Thomas Chambers first arrived at Cisco in 1991, he was already the heir apparent, the archetypal golden (albeit thinning)-haired successor. As senior vice president of worldwide operations, Chambers was John Morgridge's right-hand man. He was the engine behind the Crescendo acquisition. Along with chief strategist Ed Kozel, he played a crucial role in the development of Morgridge's business plan, the management organization, and the market positioning.

When Chambers was promoted to executive vice president in 1994, Cisco had topped the $1 billion revenue mark. In 1995, the year he was officially appointed president and CEO, the stock jumped from $33 to $89 a share, and the company made more than $2.2 billion in annual revenues. Networking was on the rise. That year he prophesied to the press that Cisco could be to networking what Microsoft had been to the software industry.

Cisco has three unique attributes that have led to its unparalleled success: its astoundingly successful acquisitions record, its highly developed use of internal technology, and its unusually tight-knit culture. John Chambers has a close hold over all three. His personality and approach are intrinsically connected to the trinity of Cisco's successes. To deconstruct Chambers is to discover Cisco. It is not too much of an exaggeration to say that the Cisco of the last few years is the corporate manifestation of John Chambers.

■ THE GENTLE MIEN

Chambers has the characteristics of a Mafia don (at least as popularized by Marlon Brando). He makes no distinction between personal values and corporate ones. He has a team of fantastically loyal people. He recognizes the significance of minor actions as an expression of larger motivations. Although he encourages team play, dissent, and discussion, he is the ultimate decision maker. (See Neil Stephenson's *Snow Crash* for a fine example of that management style in Uncle Nunzio.)[1]

Chambers's soft tenor drawl is very unassuming. He talks faster than data speeds through networks and slows down only when he is performing in front of a camera. He puts his full energy behind every sentence. He frequently jokes about being the company overhead. Then he'll launch into a full-blown plan about developing and empowering a world-class leadership team in the new Internet economy. As he speaks, his hands flutter in the air as if to help his thoughts take shape for others. His eyes have a fervent gleam as he discusses Cisco's position, the importance of its employees, or his vision for the future of the world.

His face is ruddy, but almost philosophic, as he cracks the frequent smile that has become his trademark. His eyes are childlike, a pure blue that seems to reveal constant delight at everything he says and hears. He listens well. In press photographs he often dons a serious expression and an outward gaze that seems forced. In these formal pictures, his expression is unnerving: Instead of the calm mouth and eyes expected of an industry-leading titan, the eyes are distracted and the mouth is uncharacteristically scrunched into a near frown. Chambers isn't nearly as good at looking serious and focused as he is at being intensely ebullient.

Chambers is the consummate salesperson. He started his career as one, and he continues to be one as he sells Cisco to anyone who listens: customers, employees, politicians, and stockholders. John Sidgmore, president of UUNET (the Internet subsidiary of MCI/WorldCom), one of Cisco's customers, did Chambers the favor of taking him to a Bruce Springsteen concert in 1999. Sidgmore is a big fan of the Boss, and MCI/WorldCom was a sponsor of the tour, so Sidgmore had special box seats. That wasn't enough to get Chambers to relax and enjoy the show. "He's got me up against the wall all night selling me his product!" Sidgmore laughed. "He's an incredibly competitive guy."

Chambers tells the same stories over and over again—near verbatim. "Networking is going to change everything," is his mantra. "It's going to change the way we live, work, play, and learn." He has been known to sound like an infomercial. But people listen and respond in the emphatic affirmative when, during a pep rally on the future of the Internet, he'll shout the words that have now become the company's media tagline, *"Are you ready!?"*

Unlike other technology CEOs, Chambers doesn't always seem smugly confident as he weaves his vision of the future. Indeed, he's prone to such statements as "We make Andy Grove look positively placid," meaning that he's even more fanatical than the famously paranoid Intel CEO. Chambers is also hopeful, questing, and self-deprecating. He focuses attention away from himself. In interviews, he asks reporters for their opinions. He deflects praise and regularly credits all the fine people at Cisco. When asked difficult questions, he may couch the response, but he won't avoid a direct answer.

When asked what his favorite accomplishment is, he'll retort, "My children." When asked what would be the one thing he would change about himself if he could, he'll respond, "Not having moved so many times." Chambers's image is that of the quintessential family man and overall good chap. He loves to eat Butterfingers, buttered popcorn, and steak. He was a choirboy. He married his high school sweetheart, Elaine Prater; they live in a modestly large house in Los Altos and play doubles tennis weekly. As an undergraduate, Chambers transferred from Duke to West Virginia University just to be closer to her. They have two children—a son, John Jr., and a daughter, Lindsay. Chambers never does Cisco work on Sundays, preferring to spend time with his family. His best friend, he says, is his father (also named John), a retired gynecologist who, on the side, owned a motel and restaurant where young John used to take odd jobs. Popular publicity photos feature the three generations of John Chamberses on their annual fishing trip. Chambers's mother (also a doctor), his father, and two sisters comprised a close-knit Charleston family, providing young John a childhood of cavorting about in the southern city of 52,000 and lolling on Carolina beaches during family vacations.

Surprisingly, he's also mildly dyslexic. Chambers overcame this learning disability through dedication and perseverance (although he still hates to read and dislikes written memos). After several years of tutoring and hard work, Chambers graduated second in his high school class. He relies on memory more than paper; he remembers virtually everything he hears and so never takes notes. He recites his speeches and lectures verbatim. His dislike for reading provides an even greater incentive to evolve the Internet from a text-dominated medium to a voice-integrated one.

■ EN ROUTE TO CISCO

Chambers's undergraduate years were, as he says, focused on teams. He formed social organizations and intramural teams of 5 to 300 players. Basketball was his favorite activity—the quintessential team sport. As Chambers's father once revealed to reporter Geoff Baum in an article in *Forbes ASAP,* "John played a lot of sports, but he was never the star. He liked to organize teams and expected them to win. He wouldn't have played if he didn't."[2] Chambers knew his future would somehow involve being a team leader, but didn't know exactly what profession to choose. Chambers claims that, after earning a law degree from West Virginia University and an MBA from Indiana University, his career in high tech was inspired by an interview for a sales job at IBM in 1977. In a 1999 interview with *Business Week,* he recollected that the IBM interviewer baited him with the line, "You're not selling technology, you're selling a dream."[3] Chambers nabbed the job and never left the dream-making machine of the technology industry.

➤ IBM

Still, Chambers did not exactly ride into Cisco on a string of successes. The most important lesson he learned in his previous positions was how to fail—and how to avoid failing again.

For a while, Chambers thrived as a salesperson at IBM Corporation. Within six years at the Armonk, New York, office of Big Blue, Chambers learned the ins and outs of the IBM sales and service philosophy. IBM was, Chambers remarked in retrospect, similar to what he wanted Cisco to be in that it had to move both equipment and software throughout the entire network. "Even though some people viewed IBM as a hardware company, it was largely a software company in terms of its ability to make the main-frame work in ways that its competitors could not. It was IBM's software its competitors had to run on their own systems. . . ." In the years to follow, Cisco would start pushing its software as well as its hardware to emphasize this dual nature of networking.

Chambers's training at IBM taught him to sell at multiple levels within an organization—a tack he still takes today. When he visits a potential acquisition or a large customer, Chambers will naturally talk to the president of the company. And he'll also sit down and talk technology with the person who runs the strategic business unit, as well as with the first-line manager.

But Chambers was learning from a company that was just beginning to dig its own pit and fall in. IBM would begin this way, he said; it would make a grand entrance, but would get lost once allowed inside. "What IBM did was learn to call on multiple levels," Chambers described in retrospect, "and then, over time, they forgot what got them there, and then didn't have the expertise to make the equipment run better, and then got away from their application exercise. And all of a sudden they were left with this limited relationship in some of the accounts, which they abused."[4]

According to Chambers, IBM also made another classic mistake—one he swears up and down that Cisco won't ever make—of forgetting to sell to the smaller customer. IBM didn't have much competition for the longest time, until seedlings like Computer Corporation of America, Digital Equipment, and Wang came along—followed by a wash of others, including, eventually, Cisco. "As a consequence," Chambers asserts, "people like us [Cisco] came in and took the bottom away from them. Having been there and learned from it, it offers a strong reminder on why you have to do it differently."[5]

The command-and-control architecture and draconian incentive rules also frustrated Chambers. IBM, then the top computer company in the world, had a iconic culture of conformity and loyalty. Employees adhered to a strict dress code that required young men of the 1960s to wear garters and three-piece suits instead of tie-dye. IBMers sang hagiographic tunes out of a company songbook, jingles such as "IBM, happy men/Smiling all the way/Oh, what fun it is to sell/Our products night and day"—to the tune of "Jingle Bells." The gentlemen who worked at IBM were de facto employed for life—as long as they adhered to the dress code. Although most men may have decided to throw away their garters by the time Chambers came on board in 1977, and a few women in skirts and dresses may have diversified the all-male suit-jacket aesthetic, the culture was still emphatically conservative. Salespeople were required to adhere to strict—and, to some, unfair—quotas. The pivotal moment for Chambers came when he achieved 9 out of 10 self-determined objectives, and, as a result, was told that he had failed to meet his goal. Shortly thereafter, he began interviewing elsewhere.

Not all was negative about the IBM experience, and Chambers applied to Cisco all that he could salvage from his days at Big Blue. Cisco, he says today, aspires to be like the IBM of the 1960s and 1970s (minus the garters and songbook). For one thing, Cisco aspires to make the customers trusting, loyal, and comfortable. Talking to the chief executive officer, the chief information officer, and the technology person "deep in the bowels" of the customer's company is one IBM lesson that Chambers applied to Cisco. Aggressive customer satisfaction (before IBM turned sideways) was another. "My team [at IBM] would move heaven and hell not let our customer down, and we were rewarded very well for it from that perspective. We would spend time with the president talking about where he or she was going strategically, but we balanced our role throughout."[6] At Cisco, too, Chambers sells to and supplies "across the fabric of the whole company." Chambers reiterates in almost every interview that his primary fear is that Cisco will begin to move away from its customers, as IBM did in the 1980s. At its worst, Chambers remarks, top management at IBM would tell the customers that they were wrong.

Thus, Chambers was the perfect man to respond to Morgridge's obsession with focusing on the customer with vision. As a direct result of his fear of losing the customer, Chambers invites lower-level individuals who understand the technology and the industry to speak to Cisco managers about Cisco services and products. Cisco asks them what they like about Cisco, what they don't like, and what Cisco could improve upon. Chambers actually gets livid when a Cisco employee is arrogant enough to claim to know what the customer needs better than the individual customer does. He's pinpointed that hubris as a major downfall for IBM. Chambers does his damnedest to ensure that Cisco doesn't fall prey to its own arrogance. Through the ranks at Cisco, customer satisfaction as determined by an independent survey is proportionally tied to employee bonuses. This is Cisco Lesson #1.

➤ Wang

In 1983, while Len Bosack, Sandy Lerner, and colleagues were threading wires through the Stanford campus, John Chambers took refuge in Wang Laboratories, Inc., of Billerica, Massachusetts, makers of minicomputers. Under the leadership of Dr. An Wang, Wang Laboratories grew from obscurity until, in the late 1970s and early 1980s, it was one of the companies undermining IBM's mainframes with its minicomputers and word-processing programs. A Microsoft of sorts, Wang programs were installed on virtually every office computer in the early Reagan years. Chambers's role was to run half of the company's overseas businesses.

An Wang, the founder, chairman of the board, and CEO, was, according to Chambers, the most brilliant man he ever met. Dr. Wang exercised minute control over the company—and the organizational structure reflected Wang's strategic dynamic. Over a 30-year time span, Wang Laboratories ascended, sank, and transitioned 5 times. Its last transition—the one from minicomputers to PCs—was the one that finally tripped it up. By the mid-1980s, when it became clear that PCs were here to stay, Wang's strategy for self-survival was to convert its popular word-processing software to run on PCs as well as dedicated word processors. But management feared that people wouldn't purchase Wang's more lucrative word-processing units anymore if the company transitioned to a software-dominated product base. Yet, they followed the CEO's mandate. Little did they know that other companies would come along and develop equally good PC software that would undermine Wang's market altogether.

The real crisis for Wang came in 1986. An Wang had since retired, and his son, Frederic, had taken his place. Frederic Wang maintained the same hierarchical organizational structure that his father had developed, but he lacked the same leadership skills and business insight. The command-and-control organizational structure (seven levels of management between the CEO and average product manager), as at IBM, resulted in losing track of the customer, the employee base, and, indeed, the market as a whole.

An Wang was called back from retirement to help steer the company into the black, but Wang Laboratories was unsuccessful in adapting its proprietary word-processing systems in time. In 1990, Chairman Wang asked Chambers to become senior vice president of U.S. sales and field service operations. The promotion came overnight—so quickly that Chambers knew Wang was in dire straits. An Wang died soon after Chambers's role change, and by that time, it was too late to do anything to reverse the company's downward spiral. Chambers had to oversee 5 layoffs totaling over 4,000 people. The overall staff at Wang plummeted from 35,000 to 5,500. Sales fell from $3 billion a year to $1.8 billion. The Wang stock options that once had made Chambers a paper millionaire were rendered worthless. All along he had been discouraged from cashing them in, because exercising options at Wang was viewed as a lack of faith.

Lesson #2 for Cisco, the lesson Chambers learned from Wang, was to avoid layoffs. He never wanted to do layoffs again. "It about killed me," Chambers has told more than one listener. He says—over and over again—that he would do almost anything to avoid causing another such catastrophe with employees and shareholders. Chambers invariably recalls his time at Wang in interviews. His face collapses as he discusses being the man to tell people they have lost their jobs. His simmering cheer turns dark.

From his experience at both IBM and Wang, Chambers learned to adapt *with* the flow of technology, not in resistance to it—Cisco Lesson #3. This means staying ahead of the curve. Both IBM and Wang stubbornly insisted on preserving their proprietary equipment—mainframes and word-processing systems, respectively—even after other developments in the industry had changed the playing field. In high tech, Chambers states, companies must stay ahead of the trends. If they don't, they'll destroy everything they have built and tragically disrupt the lives of their employees.

■ STARTING CISCO

Chambers quit Wang shortly after the layoffs in 1991. It was an impetuous move, because he was then unemployed. Job prospects in the depressed computer industry of the early 1990s were far and few between. He needed to contribute toward supporting his family, but, as the story goes, he didn't like the direction in which Wang was headed and decided to quit rather than hang on and hunt for a job on the sly.

Believing that he had learned more by failure than he could have by success, Chambers began looking for a leadership position at other high-tech companies. He sent out a couple of hundred resumes and sat around the house waiting for the phone to ring. He got one interview. The first month was a humbling experience for the ex-executive.

Then Chambers was told about the position of senior vice president of worldwide operations at Cisco Systems. In late 1991 Cisco employed about 500 people, with an annual sales of $183 million. John Morgridge and Don Valentine interviewed Chambers and approved. Chambers said yes, packed his family up, and moved west to San Jose. The understanding was that Chambers would be groomed for the post of CEO. John Morgridge decided around that time that he would step down from the day-to-day business of running the company, but the descent would have to be very gradual. He was ready. Morgridge explained, "They say this is a young man's game, there is the sheer physical factor of it. Long hours, on-line all the time, electronically bound to the machine 24 by 7." At 42, Chambers was prime for the position. Not that Morgridge's decision to gracefully bow out was initially accepted. Don Valentine later told *Forbes ASAP* that he had tried to talk him out of leaving. "We had the best president in the business. We wanted to do everything we could to keep him."[7] But Morgridge was adamant.

Besides, it was time to bring in some new blood. Recalls Morgridge, "It was a planned succession. If you don't do that you can have a lot of internal competition that's unhealthy because it focuses everyone internally. The mistake in our industry is not that presidents leave too early; it's that they stay too long. Ray Noorda did Novell a terrible disservice." Thus, Chambers was groomed from the get-go as the next CEO. Over the next four years as Morgridge's right-hand man, he played a key role in Cisco's acquisitions and the acquisitions strategy, the development of the overall long-term goals and objectives, and the negotiations and tech talks with the big customers. In 1994, Morgridge promoted Chambers to executive vice president of worldwide operations.

The slow transition to CEO was not without its internal glitches, no matter how carefully planned. A few members of the management team believed that Cisco needed a CEO from a more technical background—not a salesperson like Chambers. Morgridge, confident in his long-term choice for successor, asked Chambers to make more presentations to the board so as to prove to the directors that Chambers was the right person for the job. Eventually, they realized that Cisco had all the technical roots it needed, and that its necessary growth would be in Chambers's department: sales, customer support, and overall corporate image.

In 1995, only a few months after his previous promotion, John Chambers officially became CEO of Cisco and John Morgridge became chairman, after a "repotting party" to celebrate the changeover. However, Morgridge's new role wasn't to become a stationary one by any means. He became the public persona of the company in tandem with Chambers, traveling around and speaking out on issues such as education, networking, the future of the industry, and government. Morgridge's job also became that of representative for the company in Washington on issues such as NAFTA and securities litigation. Of course, he then was able find the time to pursue other loves, including biking from California to Maine with his wife and climbing mountains for various charities.

■ BUILDING MOMENTUM

Chambers's first clash with the board was fortuitous. The new CEO was prepared for his first 9-A.M. board meeting and was on his way out the door when the phone rang. A customer was on the other end, demanding to speak to him about a problem. Chambers first routed the call over to the vice president of customer advocacy, took three steps down the hall toward the conference room, thought twice, pivoted back, and took the call. He showed up 20 minutes late for the meeting. In the manner of a well-polished story, Chambers concludes, "To say my board wasn't happy was probably a fair statement. But you have to walk your talk, and when I got down there, and I shared with the board what I'd done, instead of expressing their displeasure, they said, "That was exactly the right answer."

The board warmed up to the new CEO quickly. Don Valentine has since bragged about how Cisco never lost a beat after Chambers took over. Therefore, Cisco was able to stay ahead. Chambers quickly adopted the role of CEO of the people—whether customers, employees, or shareholders. He became an advocate of the team. As a first course of action, he established a compensation system tied to team successes. Not only are leaders at Cisco compensated on customer satisfaction, but also on the quality of the teams they build. He proclaimed that he wanted to build something unique in the Valley: *teamwork*. While other CEOs might allow management to pick battles among themselves or actually wage wars against them, Chambers prides himself on not letting that happen at Cisco. "I learned a long time ago that in team sports or in business, a group working together can always defeat a team of individuals. Even if the individuals, by themselves, are each better than your team. But if you build the best team of people who play well together, then you have a dynasty."

Part of maintaining the team spirit, Chambers said, is to instill a policy of open communications. Unlike at IBM, where bureaucracy was king, or at other companies, where politicking gets one promoted, Cisco attempts to empower people with synergy. "In our organization," Chambers warned, "if I've got a leader who can't be a team player, they're gone. That doesn't mean we don't want healthy disagreement, but regardless of how well they're performing, if they can't learn over time to be part of the team and to challenge when appropriate, they really aren't going to fit into our long-term culture."[8]

➤ Decentralization

Teamwork is also critical for decentralization—Chambers's key plan for Cisco. And to decentralize the right way, Chambers would say, not only must the leaders work together, but the people who have to make it work must also work together. If they don't, decentralization doesn't work.

When Cisco was small, Morgridge centralized his cluster of core managers in the typical start-up structure. Most of the decisions were made at the top, with funnels to the engineering group, the sales group, and the service group. But with over $2 billion in annual revenue, Cisco was at the point at which Chambers could begin to decentralize management. Pete Solvik's ERP systems were up and running by this time. Cisco had to be more flexible in order to grow. Decentralization was the only way Chambers knew to grow the business at the pace he was driving it. When all the decisions have to come to the top to get made, the organization slows down to a weary grind.

The process of decentralizing Cisco had already begun with the four-step business plan that Chambers, Kozel, and Morgridge concocted the year before. Cisco would need to further decentralize in order to achieve those objectives in the coming years: (1) to assemble a broad product line to make Cisco a one-stop shop for network providers, (2) to systematize the art of acquisition, (3) to define the industrywide networking software protocols, and (4) to pick the right strategic partners. The emphasis would have to be on delegation of responsibility, teamwork, and, importantly, trust.

So Chambers created five distinct business units that reflected Cisco's major networking products and named a vice president/general manager to lead each group. Each of the five business units—workgroup, ATM high end, access, core, and IBM internetworking—had its very own marketing and engineering organization. With management thus decentralized, each division could act like a start-up within the larger organization. The technology was moving fast, and the previous centralized bureaucracy would have strangled Cisco with its bottlenecks.

Decentralizing meant a new philosophy and renewed flexibility for Cisco. As a result, many of Morgridge's vice presidents, accustomed to being among the elect few, left when Chambers took his post. Or, Chambers got rid of them.

Chambers assigned Mario Mazzola from the Crescendo acquisition to head the workgroup division. Products included LAN switching, ATM workgroup, and adapter products. The ATM high-end group, headed by a new VP named Paul Lazay, made switch products for Cisco's biggest customers. The access group, headed by Don Listwin, who had been vice president of marketing, developed standalone routers and software-based routers. Frank Marshall, who had been vice president of engineering, became head of the core group, which developed Cisco's traditional high-end backbone routers, switching technologies, and telecommunications services. Selby Wellman, a new VP and a 15-year IBM veteran, ran the IBM internetworking group out of Research Triangle Park, North Carolina. The group focused on developing routers and software products that would work with existing IBM-based computer networks as well as local- and wide-area networks.

Chambers also broke down the centralized engineering and marketing organization to be responsible for Cisco's Internetwork Operating System (IOS) and assigned Stu Phillips, who had been director of IOS, to be vice president of engineering and head of the team. Ed Kozel, who had worked with Morgridge and Chambers on the business plan and the Crescendo acquisition, got his promotion at this point, too, from vice president of business development to chief technical officer. Charles Giancarlo inherited Kozel's old title of vice president of business development and reported directly to Kozel.

Each VP would consult with Chambers on a regular basis, but was empowered with all decision-making privileges on day-to-day management. Chambers wanted to avoid the command-and-control architecture of struggling behemoths like Wang and IBM and the mindset that separates senior management from the customer and constricts progress with Byzantine processes that complicate even the most basic tasks. Micromanagement had no place at Cisco.

When he decentralized Cisco, Chambers enacted the three primary lessons learned from his experiences at IBM and Wang (focus on the customer, avoid layoffs, and adapt with the technology). Chambers wanted, above all, to be closer to the customer, so he eliminated layers of management between himself and his customers. As decision-making capabilities spread outward and downward, more and more people within the organization had the capability to make a difference. Naturally, this affected customer relations as well as Cisco's capability to adapt with the technology.

➤ Looking Ahead

Cisco's new management culture would mean fewer committees to make a decision, more people getting more recognition, and a focus on external rather than internal competition. Chambers's challenges in the years ahead would be to remain flexible through the onslaught of acquisitions and new technologies, expanding employee bases, and new relationships with businesses worldwide. The new organization would be built on change, not stability; be organized like a network, not an oppressive hierarchy; be based on interdependence with alliances, not hubristic independence; and function via new streamlined technological developments, not the old bureaucratic paper trail.

By 1995, Chambers already had his eye on the ultimate prize—to make Cisco the leader of an Internet in which traditional voice communication and cable networks would be subsumed. The last five years of the century would be crucial to Cisco. Systematically, carefully, frugally, aggressively, and politely, Chambers would need to maneuver Cisco itself into a sustaining leadership position in the networking industry.

Chapter

The Benevolent Predator (1996)

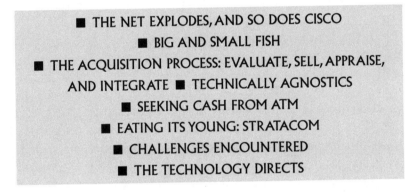

- THE NET EXPLODES, AND SO DOES CISCO
- BIG AND SMALL FISH
- THE ACQUISITION PROCESS: EVALUATE, SELL, APPRAISE, AND INTEGRATE ■ TECHNICALLY AGNOSTICS
- SEEKING CASH FROM ATM
- EATING ITS YOUNG: STRATACOM
- CHALLENGES ENCOUNTERED
- THE TECHNOLOGY DIRECTS

Nineteen ninety-six was a watershed year for Cisco. That year, Chambers reshaped Cisco by acquiring StrataCom for $4.5 billion. Cisco had acquired a number of companies before, but all were much smaller and cheaper than the 1,200-employee StrataCom. Chambers gambled by acquiring StrataCom. He had figured out how to safely snap up small networking start-ups, but StrataCom wasn't small. With the advent of the World Wide Web, all areas of networking were undergoing exponential growth. Chambers had no choice but to roll the dice. But Cisco was a well-oiled acquisitions engine, and Chambers expected StrataCom to fit right in.

■ THE NET EXPLODES, AND SO DOES CISCO

Back in 1993, when Cisco acquired Crescendo, Morgridge and Chambers took a lot of heat from the press. Commentators and pundits pronounced that the executives in charge of Cisco had lost their legendary frugality. The analysts downgraded Cisco stock severely. But by 1996, Cisco made them swallow their vitriol. Crescendo, triumphantly incorporated into the company engine, began churning out more than $500 million in revenues, up from only $10 million when it was first acquired. The phenomenal success of this, Cisco's first acquisition, greased its acquisitions track for the big purchases to come.

Cisco's success both with Crescendo and at large (the number of employees was more than doubling every year, with the head count up to 8,300 in 1996) was due to Chambers's new aggressive risk-taking acquisitions strategy in tandem with a propitious sense of timing. In 1993, the creation of the Mosaic browser at the University of Illinois and the subsequent founding of Netscape Communications gave the Internet the World Wide Web and launched an unceasing demand for networking equipment. In 1995, the National Science Foundation established the high-speed Backbone Networking Service (vBNS), which linked supercomputing centers like the National Center for Atmospheric Research (NCAR) and the National Center for Supercomputing Applications (NCSA). CompuServe, America Online, and Prodigy began providing dial-up service to the Internet. Real-Audio debuted that same year, bringing voice and music over the Web in near-real time and upping the standard for network performance. By 1996, MCI began upgrading the Internet backbone. Simultaneously, the Web-browser war between Netscape and Microsoft accelerated as new legions of Internet users began to test beta versions. WANs on college and corporate campuses became de rigueur, and the business for Cisco hardware and software escalated. Cisco starting pumping out new lines of routers and switches. To continue its heavy research and development in networks and to establish an East Coast presence, Cisco opened a facility in Research Triangle Park, North Carolina.

On top of it all, Chambers had read a Forrester research report that indicated that roughly 40 percent of all people would prefer an end-to-end vendor. The virtues of one-stop shopping, Chambers argued, were unignorable. The customers, he said, didn't want seven different sales reps calling on them. Chamber said he himself had been in that position. At home, he said, he didn't care if a problem was from the ISDN line, router, or whatever in the system network—he just wanted the problem fixed. After all, it's easier and more reliable to deal with one company that produces and services everything than with assorted parts suppliers and motley manufacturers. Chambers has since stated that Cisco had never lost a great many accounts with customers who purchased end-to-end solutions.

Chambers has always had one goal for Cisco: to become a full-service provider of Internet/telecom equipment. Over the years, Cisco tried to identify every product its customers needed and then bought the leading company in each product category. To allow a steady rate of acquisitions, Chambers had to keep Cisco stock sky-high which he did, in part, by ensuring that Wall Street viewed Cisco as the company providing the infrastrucuture or the backbone for the Internet. This way its stock mushroomed as excitement over the Internet grew.

Cisco not only was fleshing out due to the growth of the Internet—it was becoming the Internet's backbone, along with its biggest competitors: 3Com, Bay Networks, Cabletron, Digital Equipment, FORE Systems, Hewlett-Packard, and IBM.

■ BIG AND SMALL FISH

From the beginning, Cisco management understood the concept of "Internet time." It was clear that the only way for Cisco to master the market was to move faster than its competitors and become identified as the backbone of the World Wide Web—not merely another networking company. Cisco, along with 3Com and Bay Networks, was able to grow at a much faster pace than the behemoths such as HP and IBM that many, including Cisco, had expected to be the dominant players in internetworking. As Charles Giancarlo, vice president of business development, would say about Cisco's aggressive forays into new markets, "Early if not elegant." The time window into new markets was viciously small. Once a competitor established leadership in an area, that dominance would be difficult to usurp. It was best to expand as quickly as possible into other areas.

Silicon Valley was sprouting Internet start-ups by the dozens. Cisco needed a strategy to keep up with this pace of innovation. Morgridge, Chambers, and Kozel decided that the only approach was to embark on a risky strategy of acquisitions.

This decision marked a major shift in Cisco's character. The company was founded by bright technologists who invented something radically unique. Never-before-seen products established them as pioneers. But Chambers believed that in order to grow at the pace needed to remain a market leader, he would need to buy these ideas and their companies rather than relying on internal research and development. Cisco's reputation was no longer that of an innovation leader, but of a technology acquirer. These acquisitions and the innovations they brought were then the fodder for new Cisco products. The secret was to make sure the technologists stayed on after an acquisition so they could keep making innovations in their product lines. Otherwise, they would probably go off and start new companies that would compete with Cisco.

Between 1993 and April 1996, when Cisco made its $4.5 billion StrataCom acquisition, Chambers and his team acquired eight other companies: Newport Systems, Kalpana (whose products, along with Crescendo's, constituted a good part of Cisco's workgroup division), LightStream, Combinet, Internet Junction, Grand Junction, Network Translation, and TGV Software. Symbiotically, the new acquisitions bolstered Cisco's business. Kalpana brought in Ethernet switches with facilities for routers for remote network sites. Lightstream came with asynchronous transfer mode (ATM) switching and routing—a method of sending data in fixed-sized packets or "cells" across a network. CombiNet provided ISDN products and applications that were like modems, but hurried data along at a speed many times faster than traditional phone lines. Internet Junction brought in gateway software that connected desktop users with the Internet. Its Internet Junction Passport software allowed users to run IP-based applications such as Mosaic and access online resources via a network. Grand Junction made digital switches that made Ethernet networks run 10 times faster than ever imagined at the time. Network Translation made Cisco a provider of Internet firewall equipment for security-conscious network administrators. TGV brought in software products that enabled connectivity between disparate computer systems over local-area, enterprisewide, and global computing networks.

Despite its slew of acquisitions and its streamlined organization, Cisco's growth was slower than that of even younger networking companies, such as Fore and Alantec. Though common sense told Chambers that a large company can't grow as fast as a tiny start-up, he believed it was worth it for Cisco to mimic the young more nimble companies. After all, he had restructured the company so that a division competing directly with a fast-growing start-up could expand just as quickly.

Chambers understood that the larger the acquisition, the higher the chance of failure. The larger the acquired company, the more likely the danger of becoming bogged down in culture clashes, power struggles, and huge lay-offs because of redundant personnel. Cisco much preferred start-ups for their innovative drive and small size. Michelangelo Volpi, one of the VPs, described it as buying a seed and throwing soil around it. But big companies were like buying a tree, with the fear of forest fire. Chambers was paranoid about the prospect of ever having to lay off people. Because of the firm principles embodied in the Mario rule, Chambers wasn't ever willing to acquire even a small company if numerous layoffs were necessary, much less risk the higher probability of mass layoffs from a large acquisition. So when Chambers developed his acquisitions strategy, he took into account the diligent appraisal of a prospective company and the prospect of long-term security for all parties involved.

■ THE ACQUISITION PROCESS: EVALUATE, SELL, APPRAISE, AND INTEGRATE

Technology acquisitions, as mentioned in Chapter 2, are notoriously difficult to pull off. Chambers and his team developed an acquisition strategy that earned the envy of their peers. While technology acquisitions were notoriously difficult to make work organizationally, Cisco's were uniquely harmonious and equitable. Even Lew Platt, the CEO of Hewlett-Packard whose successful leadership was Chambers's model, has praised Chambers by noting that Cisco has done an exceptional job acquiring companies and operating them.

The secret was Chambers's four-step plan. Following formal criteria, Cisco engaged a battery of evaluation criteria, a simultaneous sell and appraisal process, and an integration and retention strategy. At any point before the actual stock transfer, Cisco would cease negotiations if anything were out of place. No matter how good a management team was at integration, a poor or even imperfect choice of a company would lead to failure. Similarly, a well-chosen acquisition would fail as an investment if it were not properly integrated and the new employees were not retained. The core philosophy was to aim at the future; the price tag of the acquisition was a secondary condition to Chambers, who would pay whatever it took to get the right company.

➤ Evaluation

To Chambers, an acquisition is like a marriage. (Though that would make Cisco a serial polygamist, his metaphor makes sense.) Acquisitions end in failure about as often as marriages end in divorce. No matter how hard one tries after the vows have been said, a marriage with the wrong person won't work. One date or even two isn't enough to make a lifelong commitment. So Cisco spends a lot of time courting. This way, it can choose to marry the right companies, enabling the marriage to be as painless as possible.

For Chambers, there are five keys to selecting the right acquisitions: Share a common vision, be culturally compatible, provide a quick win for shareholders, provide a long-term strategic win for all four constituencies, and be geographically desirable.

Share a Common Vision

The business development team at Cisco liked calling potential acquisitions the "Cisco Kids." More than an unavoidable pun, the term reflected the mandate to find companies that would resemble Cisco in five to six years. They were mostly interested in Bosack-and-Lerner-style start-ups: fast-growing, focused, entrepreneurial companies. Cisco looked for an excellent team, especially in technical and marketing areas. They were only interested in excellence—the prospect of an accelerated momentum.

Even being a high-octane start-up wasn't enough to be

a Cisco Kid. The prospective company had to be moving in the same direction as Cisco. Chambers looked to see if their visions were the same—about where the industry was going, what role each company wanted to play in the industry. If not, he knew that the two would remain factions forever at war. One exception he allowed were differences in technology visions or industry visions. But the product strategies of the two companies had to complement each other, rather than compete. Cisco's philosophy about technology had to be shared.

Not too many companies would qualify. In fact, Cisco aborted about as many acquisitions as it made. It may seem that being this choosy is a luxury one can't afford in a fast-moving industry, but Chambers knew that only a perfect fit could have a reasonable chance of success.

Be Culturally Compatible

Chambers differentiated between sharing a common vision and being culturally similar, his second criteria. Any acquisition had to able to work with Chambers's management, as he intended that the acquired executives would become part of that management. Though it was admittedly hard to define, Chambers insisted that the chemistry had to be right. Bad chemistry with the management team would be the first deal-breaker. The people acquired would have to be able to enjoy working at Cisco. Chambers would analyze the new company's management philosophy, determine the solidity of its management team, and, from there, determine how well the new company would meld with Cisco's culture.

This requirement came out of a previous acquisition mistake Cisco made. In 1994, the company acquired LightStream, a Billerica, Massachusetts, company purchased in order to gain an early entry into the asynchronous transfer mode (ATM)—another networking protocol—market. Lightstream was a prime example of an East Coast academic culture of companies that had sprung from MIT.

This did not blend well with the almost fanatical pragmatism of Cisco's Silicon Valley style. Tensions had been brewing with LightStream for some time. Soon after the LightStream acquisition, a tight cultural fit and extra care with integration became higher priorities.

Provide a Quick Win for Shareholders

The third necessary condition in the evaluation stage of an acquisition was that the prospective company had to immediately deliver a positive return. Chambers knew that acquisitions are always closely scrutinized by the shareholders.

The pace of the industry meant that Cisco could not afford to give up a quick return with every acquisition. Chambers began comparing the rate of development in the industry to dog years. If one calendar year is equivalent to seven years of normal growth, each acquisition would have to contribute to Cisco's bottom line at an unbelievable pace. No matter how successful previous acquisitions had been, each new one had to produce a quick win. Chambers disliked companies that were more than a few months away from delivering a product to the marketplace. However, Chambers was at times willing to pay extraordinary prices for acquisitions, which meant that there was no way these investments could pay off quickly. The overarching philosophy was to look toward the future—buy a company that is critical to the future marketplace of Cisco customers no matter what the price.

Provide a Long-Term Strategic Win for All Four Constituencies

Chambers and the board demanded long-term benefits from acquisitions. Chambers knew that each acquisition had to satisfy all of Cisco's constituencies: its shareholders, customers, employees, and business partners. The root of Cisco's strategy was to benefit all the constituencies. By carefully asking if an acquisition would benefit everyone in the long run, Cisco avoided making deals for short-sighted reasons.

Chambers disliked making acquisitions that did not benefit the employees of the acquired company. Employees from acquisitions were particularly pumped when told that their stock options would continue to be vested at the acquired company's old rate, but for Cisco stock. Cisco was not going to acquire a company, no matter how good the financials looked, only to lay off its people.

Be Geographically Desirable

Finally, Cisco only wanted to acquire companies that were geographically desirable. Of the first nine companies Cisco acquired, eight were in Santa Clara County's Silicon Valley, next door to Cisco's San Jose headquarters. Only LightStream, acquired in December 1994, was located elsewhere, in the heart of the Route 128 tech corridor outside Boston, Massachusetts. The other area where Cisco would consider making acquisitions was near its East Coast headquarters, opened in 1993 in Research Triangle Park, near Raleigh and Durham, North Carolina. Later, as Cisco expanded worldwide, small acquisitions would be made at strategic points across the globe.

If Cisco were to do an acquisition of a large company, it would most likely have to be located in Silicon Valley. Chambers's attitude was that if he had a problem, he didn't want to have to board an airplane to solve it.

➤ The Cisco Sell

When Cisco decides that it may want to acquire a company, it takes a decidedly understated approach. With a godfatherlike concern for politeness, Cisco executives emphasize the benefits of working together before and after the deal. Negotiations take place at lunch whenever possible. Handshakes and familiarity rather than hostile takeover define the tone of the relationship between Cisco and the acquired company.

The first few Cisco acquisitions were handled directly by Chambers, the expert salesperson, from start to finish. Once a more formal acquisitions team was in place, however, one of his lieutenants would make the first move. But Chambers was the one who always stepped in at the end to close the deal. The process generally began when Charles Giancarlo or Michelangelo Volpi, vice presidents of business development, or Ed Kozel, chief technology officer, initiated discussions with the CEO of the target company. The designated officers had the power to take discussions to the penultimate level.

Cisco would approach a prospective Cisco Kid CEO with, basically, kid gloves. All engagements were as friendly and relaxed as possible in a high-tech buyout. Most important, by Cisco's moral code, every deal was required to be carefully tailored to the interests of the acquired company. No one-size-fits-all approach for Cisco. As Barbara Beck, vice president of human resources, said, many departments at Cisco would be involved in the acquisition: human resources, finance, business development, engineering, and legal. Cisco never had an unfriendly takeover because acquisitions were designed to accommodate the people first, then the product. After all, as Beck noted, the only way an acquisition works is if the people want to come.

Krish Ramakrishnan, CEO of Internet Junction, described his company's acquisition by Cisco in 1995 as a very pleasant one. First, Cisco CTO Ed Kozel, who was managing business development at the time, contacted Internet Junction's headquarters in Mountain View, California:

Cisco approached us. The CTO came and had lunch, told us about his vision and wanted to hear ours. Then I had a one-hour lunch with Chambers at Cisco.

John put me at ease. What he was trying to figure out was whether we would be successful in this environment. He asked me about my vision for the company. John's opinion is that if the people fit, everything else would work out. At the end of the lunch there was a handshake and the deal was done in a couple of days. We made a deal, not like what you'd imagine when you're trying to sell a company. I was interviewing for a job rather than selling my company.[1]

The hard work Cisco's acquisition team was doing behind the scenes to understand Internet Junction and its people is evident from this glowing description. Equally important is how Ramakrishnan expected to be working for Cisco as the acquisition was hammered out. With the personal touch, and mutual respect, Chambers acquired Internet Junction. Chambers knew how to get what he wanted: the product and the people.

Cisco's acquisition of Grand Junction, also in September 1995, was more complicated. Grand Junction had been founded in 1992 by Howard Charney, Jack Moses, and Larry Birenbaum, all from 3Com. Charney had decided to leave 3Com soon after its board decided to dump his friend, 3Com cofounder Bob Metcalfe.

Grand Junction's first plan was to take the company public. In the summer of 1995, the company hired Goldman Sachs to begin the process for an initial public offering. But in July, Goldman Sachs approached Cisco VP Charlie Giancarlo, knowing Cisco's reputation of paying top dollar for innovative companies. Grand Junction was at the forefront of *Fast Ethernet* technology, which allowed local-area networks to run 10 times faster than its predecessor, Ethernet. The LAN switching market was very hot; companies like Fore Systems and Alantec, which went public in 1994, were worth about $350 million each. Cisco decided to take a look. Giancarlo was led to believe by Goldman Sachs that an acquisition would be in the $200 million range.

Grand Junction satisfied Cisco's acquisition criteria. A fellow Silicon Valley company, it shared Cisco's vision and culture. Its well-experienced management team had new products ready for release. The purchase of Grand Junction would allow Cisco to effectively counter its competitors in desktop switching and Fast Ethernet over the long term.

Cisco VP Mario Mazzola, a long-time friend of Howard Charney, joined Giancarlo in a visit to Grand Junction. Charney and Mazzola had a warm meeting; the former was grateful that Cisco sent someone to talk to him who had been brought into the company under similar circumstances. Mazzola gave the green light.

Cisco made an offer of about $200 million, Giancarlo's original estimate. Grand Junction and Goldman Sachs looked at the valuations of competing public companies and asked for more than $300 million. Chambers himself then became involved in the negotiations. Without making threats, he pointed out why joining Cisco was a wise decision. Cisco's stock was skyrocketing as its position of market leader solidified. Charney, above all, wanted his products to win, and Cisco's muscle could make that happen. As the month progressed, Grand Junction watched the values of rival companies rise. Charney knew he could continue to ask for more from Cisco as Grand Junction's potential value rose. At the end of the month, Chambers offered 5 million shares for Grand Junction. At the time, those shares were worth $325 million, a better sum than the original offer, but still too low for Charney and Goldman Sachs.

At that point, Charney questioned the real value of an acquisition. He had promised many of his 85 employees that Grand Junction would go public. Some employees had left Cisco to join his company, and they wouldn't welcome a deal that put them back where they started. On the other hand, he knew how difficult it would be to succeed in the long run against companies like Cisco, 3Com, and Bay Networks—the latter of which was also vying to acquire Grand Junction. Charney could not be sure that Grand

Junction could compete successfully with its existing or new competitors. After all, the networking industry had become increasingly concentrated in recent years as a result of consolidations. Bigger, fatter competitors could devote significantly greater resources to the development and marketing of new rival products. So, at the last moment, he deferred to Cisco. The two companies held final talks on September 16. Cisco reiterated its standing offer of $325 million. Charney told them his final terms: the 5 million shares of Cisco stock, at that point worth about $346 million. Cisco accepted those terms, and Grand Junction was acquired. By the time the acquisition officially closed, the value of the deal rose to about $400 million.

➤ Cisco's Appraisal

Cisco would appraise a potential acquisition while giving it the hard sell. The acquisition team performed due diligence to ensure that each acquisition choice was a good one. This team, drawn from every major department of Cisco, determined whether Cisco could integrate the upper management and the line-level employees successfully. They paid special attention to financial and employment details that could explode into large problems if not found at this stage.

Chambers emphasized that critically examining acquisitions was central to Cisco's acquisition success. The acquisition team would spend about two weeks in a "war room" reexamining the company to see if it did, in fact, satisfy Cisco's guidelines. Each of the five evaluation criteria was retested from the perspective of every department. The team made the recommendation whether to go through with the acquisition. Chambers admitted that at this point he killed nearly as many acquisitions as he made.

Human resources examined the organization and issues concerning all its personnel, not just the managers. Their mandate was to ensure that Cisco would have a fighting chance of retaining all the new employees. They reconfigured stock deals to keep engineers; one acquisition was scuttled when they discovered massive pension liabilities that would cause the actual cost of the acquisition to rise far past Cisco's desired price point.

As stock options were the primary incentive for Cisco and the entire networking industry, the due-diligence team spent much of their time dealing with stock equity. Cisco would take note of how equity was distributed in the candidate company. They knew that inequitable distribution pointed to problems, to an executive team that didn't value its employees. Stock options were also the primary incentive Cisco had to keep employees in the company. Until employees stayed with Cisco long enough for their stock options to be vested, those options were worth little. Therefore, Cisco didn't do a deal if the candidate company had accelerated vesting, preferring "golden handcuffs." Cisco stock, as it steadily rose, locked unvested employees firmly in place.

In the end, when the due-diligence team thought that the acquisition was a good idea, the final okay was quickly given. For the sake of streamlined brevity, the full board, made up of other Cisco executives and industry hotshots, was not involved in most acquisitions. Chambers, Morgridge, and Valentine alone made the decision; they convinced the board that an acquisition was just another everyday business decision. Cisco tried to keep the terms of its acquisitions as simple as possible. Chambers strove to keep the acquisition process as simple, fast, and foolproof as possible.

But Cisco's work only began with the acquisition.

➤ Integration and Retention

Cisco had to retain the right people if the acquisition was to succeed for the long term. Elsewhere in the datacom industry, the defection rate of acquired employees was as high as 40 percent. At Cisco, employees were, in fact, *less* likely to leave if they came from an acquisition than if they had been directly hired. Cisco did all the right things to not only get what it wanted, but to keep what it needed.

Because the primary asset of Cisco's acquisitions was the people, it would be downright foolish not to do everything to keep them. Chambers once calculated that Cisco paid anywhere from $500,000 to $2 million per person in an acquisition.

Cisco integrated new employees quickly and thoroughly. As Ramakrishnan noted, "It's the people who get integrated first, not the product." New roles and titles were immediately announced. VP Selby Wellman once explained that when Cisco acquires a company, they never tell them, "We'll leave you alone." Instead, they tell them, "We'll change everything." Chambers's philosophy on employee retention is that Cisco tells employees up front what Cisco's plans are because trust is everything. Employees find it hard not to fall in love with Cisco stock options. New employees become part of future acquisition teams.

Sometimes Cisco would have the newly acquired teams of engineers work next door to Cisco senior management to build rapport in the first few weeks. However, as Solvik did with the IT budgets, central management allowed the engineering teams to make decisions on their own, acting as free-standing units of a company bound by a common vision and strong but flexible central management.

To keep all the acquired employees, Cisco knew it had to keep the top executives. As when a queen ant leaves the colony, the departure of the executive leadership from an acquisition often leads to the disappearance of its workers. The executives Cisco acquired were all of a common breed: single-minded, dynamic entrepreneurs. Entrepreneurs as a class are dissatisfied with working in large corporations; it's part of what drives them to start new companies.

Cisco retained entrepreneurs by giving them constant challenges and opportunities. Founding executives like Howard Charney (from Grand Junction), Krish Ramakrishnan (from Internet Junction), and Charlie Giancarlo (from Kalpana) necessarily moved down the totem pole from CEO slots when they joined Cisco. But they stayed. "They gave me a chance to play a major role," explained Giancarlo, who was offered the opportunity to run Cisco's business development and acquisitions.[2] Ramakrishnan, the engineering entrepreneur, appreciated the opportunities to explore new technologies. "Our stock has been vested so we could leave any time, but we want to continue to do new things at Cisco." Charney, also made a vice president of engineering, discovered that there were in fact benefits to Cisco's patchwork of acquisitions. "What I really love about this place is the contest of ideas. Because we have people from different companies, there are different approaches to solving problems. That creates an atmosphere of excitement that even the best small company can't duplicate."[3] Moreover, Charney enjoyed other aspects of being part of Cisco. "I'm still running an operation whose mission is managing lives and technology, but I don't worry about cash flow. I don't worry about having enough R&D money to keep up with the big boys. We *are* the big boys."[4]

■ TECHNICALLY AGNOSTICS

As Cisco grew to almost 8,000 employees in 1996, Cisco crept into new territories. Each acquisition generally represented a strategic, if minuscule, step away from Cisco's core business of routers. Before 1996, over 80 percent of Cisco's business still came from the router market, but Chambers was cruising full steam ahead in his desire to diversify. One of his favorite mantras is that of technical agnosticism: "The companies that get into trouble are those that fall in love with 'religious technologies,' " he says. "The key to success is having a culture with the discipline to accept change and not fight the religious wars."

Just as the speed of computers doubled every 18 months (Moore's law), so did the size of the networking industry. Some companies chose to be insular and clung to one technology. Cisco chose to make diverse acquisitions. As Chambers declared, "When a customer said to us, we're thinking about buying one of these whowhatsits, we often bought the company that did the whowhatsits." Cisco made a point of not caring whether a product was invented under Cisco's roof. It just cared whether it would be the next best thing that would push the company forward.

Chambers wanted to bring extended and diverse networking options into its Internetworking Operating System (IOS). Cisco was attempting to formalize all the software that ran on its equipment into a coherent IOS package. According to Chambers, customers were beginning to seek a strategic provider to provide an end-to-end solution for their respective networks. This software package complemented Cisco's hardware packages. Once users bought into Cisco's IOS, it would be easier for them to extend or update their networks with Cisco equipment than with a competitor's.

■ SEEKING CASH FROM ATM

The ATM market was of burgeoning interest to Cisco in the mid-1990s. ATM, a dedicated-connection switching technology, organizes data—from e-mails to voice to video to imaging—into uniform 53-byte cells or packets and transmits it over a signal. Hardware-based, and therefore faster than routers, ATM was a vision of better, brisker data relay. ATM's greatest strength was that it allowed digital emulation of traditional phone networks. If all the kinks were worked out, ATM could be the bridge between data communications and telecommunications. That would be big. But the kinks were big: The technology was very complicated, imperfect, and too expensive for most networking situations. Moreover, combining ATM with the Internet by stuffing IP packets into ATM cells was unwieldy and difficult. Still, advances were being made every day. Cisco had already acquired Kalpana and LightStream for their ATM products, but the market was moving fast, with more and more advanced versions of the switches popping up all the time.

Back in 1993, Cisco, StrataCom, and AT&T announced an agreement to collaborate on the definition of standards and the development of products and services for ATM. Expectations were lofty. Their vision for ATM, as posited in the AT&T news release, was to "bring about a world in which the distinctions between local and wide area networks disappear . . . a world in which computers, large and small, have global connectivity to multiple information platforms as easily as making a call next door, and many times faster. . . . It is a world where distance ceases to be a consideration, and bandwidth bottlenecks are no longer an issue. It is a world where networking is the unifying technology."[5]

While this news release could have defined the vision of networking in general, it demonstrated that Cisco and its partners identified ATM as a key part of that future. The networking world was abuzz with the potential of ATM. Ed Kozel, chief technology officer, publicly announced that no existing Cisco technologies of the time would necessarily be usurped by ATM. As dedicated as Cisco was to preserving the existing router dominion (and keeping its customer base assured of its enduring relevance), the virtues of ATM were too enticing to ignore, and Chambers and his team were determined to cover all bases of the sprawling networking industry.

They had already made a small foray into the market with LightStream Corporation, which was only a year old at the time. Prior to the acquisition, LightStream netted only $1.5 million in hardware revenue. One year later, it made $45 million. Even so, LightStream was lightweight compared to ATM incumbents like StrataCom and Cascade. LightStream was only at the campus enterprise level; it sold ATM switches for use in small to midsized corporate networks. This did not fulfill Cisco's desire to sell equipment that could be used in the global Internet. And, as Chambers later admitted, LightStream was about two generations away from producing the products that StrataCom and Cascade, Cisco's greatest competitors in the field, were selling. Chambers quickly realized that LightStream was not strong enough to compete in the ATM market—which, as Chambers later conceded, had accelerated a lot faster than anticipated.

Before 1995, customers were telling Cisco that Fast Ethernet should be its primary objective before ATM—and the decision was right at the time; Fast Ethernet outsold ATM at least 5 to 1. Cisco, in fact, had developed a way to speed up Ethernet to 100 megabits per second, a strategy that could have stalled or stifled the implementation of ATM, which was running as fast as Ethernet, if not faster. ATM prevailed in markets particularly suited to its strengths, such as the telephone and banking industries, where reliability and security are primary needs.

By 1995, Chambers had to put Cisco on a new course. Cisco's customers were demanding to combine their wide-area networking requirements with LAN-to-LAN requirements—providing even greater flexibility to distributed parties. Fast Ethernet was great LAN technology, but wasn't designed for wide-area networking. The customers wanted the best WAN technology, and that meant frame relay and, particularly, ATM. They were letting Cisco know that while they liked its direction with LightStream, they were wary of buying ATM products from Cisco because they feared that it was not going to have a comfortable, confidence-inspiring market share in the next 12 or 18 months. They feared that their purchases would be obsolete before they knew it.

By end of 1995, Cisco started to look hungrily at ATM and frame-relay producers StrataCom and Cascade. Chambers knew that if Cisco wasn't one of the first couple of players into a market with a strong product, it would be very difficult for it to ever become the number-one or number-two player. When asked why Cisco didn't pursue development in ATM earlier and more aggressively, Chambers replied that Cisco had been growing research and development almost 100 percent year after year. To grow it much faster than that would have been exceedingly difficult. From studying the General Electric strategy, Chambers knew that being number one or two was crucial to playing the game at all. Because Cisco was a latecomer in the ATM marketplace, Chambers's choice on that base was to hit hard or not at all.

■ EATING ITS YOUNG: STRATACOM

Maintaining an emphatically agnostic stance on the "holy wars" of ATM versus frame relay versus IP, Cisco decided to sell all options, and, as Chambers advertised, allow Cisco's customers to choose the combinations they wanted. It was Chambers's view that customers would increasingly select vendors based on how they integrated their products with existing and future technologies. With beefed-up capacities to supply ATM and frame relay technology, Cisco could be the clear choice for one-stop shopping for all hybrids of networking solutions. With LightStream's ATM product line progressing steadily—but too slowly—Cisco decided that being number one or two required a serious acquisition.

"When something changes faster than we anticipated, or we make some other mistake, then we adjust very quickly and don't spend a lot of time with the 'Not Invented Here' syndrome, trying to protect our decisions of two years ago," declared Chambers. Chambers was trying to compete with the fast growth of small companies as well as trying to beat the large companies in the ATM sphere. Chambers found that LightStream couldn't give Cisco the competitive edge it needed, so Cisco had to swallow a little humble pie and risk a larger acquisition. In the process, Cisco had to stunt the growth of LightStream and pare down its product line to make room. One of Cisco's strengths is the ability to eat its young in an aggressive market. It is this willingness to sacrifice parts of itself for long-term advantages that separates a company like Cisco from the rest of the pack.

In 1995, the quandary came down to StrataCom or Cascade. Cisco already had an equity investment in Cascade; a few years earlier, in a move that Chambers called simultaneously an "offensive and defensive move in a market segment that we were just beginning to understand," it had put in $2.9 million. Wellfleet, a competitor at the time (it later merged with SynOptics), had been developing a frame-switching product that could have taken off to Cisco's detriment. Cisco's investment in Cascade, which also manufactured frame-switching products, was an insurance policy of sorts. Although the threat of the Wellfleet product never actually materialized, the frame-switching market grew tangibly, and Cisco's investment in Cascade turned a profit of over $200 million. As Morgridge hedged, "Just because you have equity doesn't mean you're going to buy. It could be a partnership or internal development. Even when we're negotiating to acquire someone we keep more than one option open." The equity bit didn't ultimately affect the decision. But Cascade had a few strikes against it: It was dramatically more expensive, had entered into a joint development agreement with IBM in March 1995, and didn't share Cisco's outlook on the future of networking.

After all was balanced and deliberated, StrataCom had the most points in its favor: It was a market leader in frame relay and ATM (with 40 and 22 percent of the market share, respectively); it could bring wide-area networking and LAN-to-LAN internetworking closer together; the wins looked good for employees, investors, customers, and partners; the cultural chemistry worked; and the location (San Jose) was right. Every box on the acquisitions strategy checklist was marked. Because Cisco and StrataCom were neighbors, Chambers added, "You could look the employees in the eye and say, 'You know, we're not going to lay anybody off.' And it's real important in acquisitions to be very credible with your people. If you're going to lay people off, you tell them [on] day one. And not only are we not going to lay them off, we have 600 openings. Strata-Com has 100 openings. We're within a couple minutes drive of each other."[6]

The ATM and frame-relay industry was still booming as the StrataCom deal was initiated. Chambers declared that StrataCom was attractive to Cisco because of its drive to keep up with the demands of the Internet and, there-fore, to drive technology toward preventing the Internet from bogging down. Chambers put his chip on a combina-tion of wide-area switching and routing. With StrataCom's experience in very high-end WAN switches for data, ATM, and frame relay, Cisco stood a good chance in the market. Moreover, with StrataCom, Cisco would acquire not only the necessary technology but also marketing clout, due to StrataCom's close relationship with the regional Bell hold-ing companies. With the additional market value of Strata-Com, Cisco would be able to acquire more and more expensive companies over time.

Chambers decided to broker this deal personally. He took StrataCom CEO Dick Moley out for dinner in a private room at the Westin Hotel in Santa Clara, where he placed a semiformal offer on the table. Less than two weeks later, Chambers and Moley made the joint announcement and Cisco divested its stock in Cascade. Cascade was later ac-quired by Cisco competitor Ascend, which, in turn, was acquired by Cisco competitor Lucent . . . but that's a story for a later chapter.

The two companies agreed to a stock-swap agreement in which shares of Cisco stock would be exchanged for all outstanding shares, options, and warrants of StrataCom stock on a one-to-one basis. Cisco's stock price on Friday, April 19, 1996, the day of the swap, was $47.75, adding up to a $4.5 billion deal—Cisco's largest acquisition until 1999. Cascade, meanwhile, announced an acquisition of its own, that of Arris Networks for $145.3 million in common stock.

Engineers and salespeople in networking inevitably seemed to work for larger and larger companies. Chambers didn't anticipate the same phenomenal *monetary* return as Cisco had realized from Crescendo. However, he knew that StrataCom would immediately put money back into Cisco's coffers, because StrataCom was an established company with established product lines. The acquisition wasn't about raw growth potential alone; it was about the people and facilities. The new infusion of networking technologies made Cisco the first vendor to provide advanced network infrastructure for intranets and the Internet, and the only vendor able to provide end-to-end connectivity across public, private, and hybrid networks.

StrataCom employees, as promised, kept their jobs, and Dick Moley became senior vice president and general manager of a newly wrought WAN business unit. In addition, Moley cashed in from the acquisition, with a $22 million profit in stock. In a trend that indicates that stock is ultimately more valuable and profitable than a high salary, StrataCom's 14-member board of directors and top officers instantly earned a combined $45.9 million paper profit from the buyout. Unlike the historical mergers and acquisitions between Wellfleet and SynOptics, 3Com and ChipCom, and Fore and Alantec, whose stocks dropped an average of 14 percent in the week after the acquisition announcements, Cisco's stock went up 10 percent in the week following the StrataCom announcement. This, to Chambers, was an affirmation that the market understood what Cisco was doing. The elated CEO broadcast in interviews and press releases that Cisco was the first company that was able to play all the way from the desktop to the central office, now that StrataCom was part of Cisco. StrataCom products were to be incorporated as part of the family of Cisco's IOS, and Cisco would incorporate StrataCom's traffic and quality-of-service software in its own routers and switches. Chambers and his executive core combined StrataCom and Cisco in a record-breaking 90 days.

Of course, despite Chambers's optimistic promotion, and the optimistic stock prices, dubious speculation about the effect of the StrataCom purchase abounded in the marketplace. According to analysts, the acquisition soon created confusion and a backlash in Cisco's product line that initially hurt its ATM positioning. Although Cisco posted a statement regarding the StrataCom acquisition on its Web site to assure inquirers that Light-Stream's products, the LightStream 2020 and 1010, did not overlap with StrataCom's product families, Cisco discontinued the LightStream 2020 ATM switch a few months after the acquisition. The changeover clearly upset Light-Stream buyers, who were stuck with a discontinued product. The company formerly known as LightStream, once a promising new division of Cisco, stopped growing strongly. Instead of being the core of Cisco's ATM strategy (as Crescendo had become the core of Cisco's LAN switching), LightStream became a mere adjunct to StrataCom. Cisco needed to regain its balance quickly.

■ CHALLENGES ENCOUNTERED

John Morgridge reflected on the StrataCom acquisition, "[It] was good because we gained insight on the unique challenges of doing a big deal versus a small one. We felt pretty good with the small deals. Whenever you feel like that you better watch out." StrataCom, Cisco's largest acquisition until 1999, gave Chambers and his core ample opportunity to learn important lessons fast. The StrataCom integration challenges included channeling new technology, potential customer discontent, and competitor animosity.

➤ Channeling New Technology

Despite all the publicity boasting that it took only 90 days to integrate StrataCom into Cisco, Morgridge later admitted otherwise. "It took a lot longer to assimilate StrataCom, a lot of technology our force field had to learn. They were right next to us and we did a great job in integrating manufacturing, services, purchasing." Among Cisco's greatest feats was developing bug-free software for StrataCom's platforms and fully incorporating it into the IOS with troubleshooting, management, and policy-routing features. Yet another internal challenge was to get the company as a whole to embrace ATM. Despite Cisco's insistence on technological agnosticism, it had been emphatically biased toward IP. Blending the two networking cultures was the first hurdle to overcome.

Morgridge declared that the divergent products created a great deal of initial confusion. He related to journalist Southwick that "Leveraging their technology through our [sales] channel was a much more daunting task." One commentator complained that StrataCom's products, which had once competed against Cisco's routers, would effectively become "lobotomized" when they were incorporated into Cisco's IOS.[7] Barry Eggers, then director of business development for Cisco and head of the Cisco-StrataCom transition effort, announced a postacquisition sales strategy that would assign an entire sales account team to focus on different aspects on the infrastructure network, the internal network, and opportunities for reseller agreements. Cisco also announced plans to provide higher levels of customer support services to maintain reliability standards and help customers get systems set up. It set up a 5- to 7-day technical training program for a handful of sales channels (50 within a 2-month period) to ensure that it would be able to provide the proper technical support for the StrataCom products.

It is said that the toughest sell of StrataCom equipment may have been to Cisco's native sales force, which numbered 1,800 at the time. Despite all the talk about a pan-theistic IOS, the router salespeople were accustomed to Cisco's lucrative high-end routers, which netted $100,000 to $200,000 commissions, and they weren't necessarily eager to change that. An entire StrataCom switch started at a price of $24,000—clearly netting a much lower commission. Incorporating newer, cheaper alternatives would require new incentives and an altered mindset for Cisco employees.

StrataCom came with a 200-person sales organization of its own. But to make matters worse, many of those salespeople weren't willing to stick around to make things better. To add fuel to the fire, Barry Eggers, director of business development, announced that the company would explore different ways of shortening the sales window on products. "That," a reporter for *InternetWeek* commented, "isn't sitting well with StrataCom's sales force, which is well-versed in the slow, methodical, year-long sale to a carrier."[8] As successful as Cisco was in keeping positions and opportunities open for the 1,200 ex-StrataCom employees, Morgridge conceded that Cisco wasn't successful in integrating StrataCom's sales force. "Sales organizations have a zero-sum game mentality."

➤ Potential Customer Discontent

Chambers claimed that StrataCom's sales had increased after the acquisition, from $90 million to $100 million in quarterly sales and to $160 million in booking for products and services. In a public statement, he declared that StrataCom had more new customers in the first quarter than it had had in all of 1995, adding that the number of customers in the second quarter was up 25 percent over that of the first quarter of fiscal year 1997. But critics were quick to be suspicious of any braggadocio. Other industry leaders claimed that Cisco was trying to mask failed expectations and stretching its statistics by including a lot of bookings—and by counting sales of Light-

Stream ATM switches and other products in StrataCom's totals.

Critics were quick to point out that the elimination of the LightStream 2020 would cause customer discontent. Shortly after the StrataCom acquisition in 1996 *Internet-Week* featured an article on the "incredible shrinking industry" of telecommunications. The writer posed the question to *InternetWeek*'s readers: Will the industry be better served by a few Cisco-like megacarriers and equipment suppliers? Answering his own question in the negative, the writer proffered the example of Cisco's LightStream 2020. "If I were a customer, Cisco's decision would make me rethink its commitment to any product it is about to sell me."[9] Customers with recently installed LightStream 2020s were considerably angered and disappointed. To compensate for past and future losses, Don LeBeau, Cisco's senior vice president of worldwide sales, announced a generous investment protection plan for customers who wanted to migrate to StrataCom platforms. In addition, Cisco's customer service placated recent Light-Stream customers with a promise that it would compensate them for the full value of the old switches when applied toward new equipment, and would provide the necessary assistance and training. Nevertheless, as one Lexis-Nexus telecommunications engineer remarked, "It will still mean a lot of wasted time and training as well as inconveniences and downtime for our users."[10]

Among the hurdles in making new acquisitions work that Cisco had to jockey were the natural demands put on a one-stop provider. Sales cycles, despite efforts to the contrary, tend to lengthen. Customer service must be 99-plus percent available. With Cisco as a one-stop producer, its customers would have to swear allegiance to it and sacrifice potentially better deals elsewhere. Daniel Smith, president and CEO of competitor Cascade, voiced his challenge soon after the acquisition. "A carrier would have to turn its back on more than half the marketplace," he said. "That's a recipe for unprofitability."[11]

➤ Competitor Animosity

There was a dark side to Cisco's strategy of acquiring *every* equipment vendor that could help it build the growing skeleton of the Internet. Competitors began to worry that Cisco was becoming a monopoly. Shortly after the Strata-Com acquisition, 3Com, Bay Networks, and IBM formed a Network Interoperability Alliance (NIA), in part to combat a feared monopoly by Cisco. A director at Forrester Research voiced the ethos of the NIA when he derided Cisco's Internetwork Operating System and issued an implicit warning to Cisco's vendors. "Third parties know they will lose their market to Cisco eventually if they buy into the IOS story. Next thing you know, Cisco is in your face with a piece of equipment that does what yours did."[12]

The NIA's agenda was to promote a common set of open specifications for building integrated networks. Its strategy was to pursue testing of appropriate products from all three companies in the alliance to ensure robust interoperability. The NIA also courted Microsoft, Netscape Communications, and Novell.

Cisco was to refine its integrative skills and strategies in the megaacquisition years ahead (as discussed in later chapters), not least by simply forging ahead despite gripes and grumbles. As Barry Eggers summarized, "A common mistake in acquisitions is to get too inward focused on the organization, and then lose perspective on the market."[13]

■ THE TECHNOLOGY DIRECTS

Cisco's aggressive acquisition strategy was and still is inextricably bound with the technology it sells. As technologies grow, as the NIA knew and feared, they tend to converge in order to maintain compatibility. The old shared-media days were over and gone. No longer could a customer plug one brand of hub into another brand of router.

By the end of the year, Cisco was well on its way to becoming the major one-stop supplier of end-to-end networking products. It had 21.9 percent of the worldwide networking market, compared to 3Com at 12.8 percent, Bay Networks at 11.6 percent, IBM at 8.3 percent, and Cabletron at 6.0 percent. The rest of the market was fragmented, with no splinter boasting more than 3.3 percent. About 80 percent of the routers that comprised the Internet's backbone were Cisco routers. Cisco was also responsible for 73 percent of IBM Systems Network Architecture (SNA) equipment, 63 percent of branch access devices, 38 percent of frame-relay devices, and 35 percent of LAN switches. Its net sales in 1996 were $4.1 billion, thanks to its 8,259 employees.

As the industry shifted leaving the usual wake of upheavals and impasses, Cisco aimed to remain the market leader and shaper. Internet growth continued to increase, causing severe traffic jams. As a result, some Internet service providers found a solution in combining more economical ATM switches with expensive, powerful routers, thereby combining ATM and IP service. Cisco was there to provide both. "With a combination of IP routing and ATM, we can define the Internet of the future," Chambers announced. The StrataCom acquisition, for all intents and purposes, was a great success. In order to fill continuously emerging gaps in its own product lines, Cisco would continue to advance with 10 to 12 acquisitions per year, defining and refining its strategy with each union.

Chapter

A Day in the Life

To join Cisco is to join the Cisco clan. Cisco workers are widely known as productive, happy, and driven. They're also completely enveloped by the Cisco way. The devout happiness of people who spend nearly all of their energy just for Cisco has led to intimations that Cisco resembles a big cult. If Cisco is a cult, then it's pretty benevolent in sharing its success with its members. Moreover, it's all the more impressive for what it is not: Cisco is not religious about technology, or attitude, or process. The two things Cisco holds dear are happy customers and employee productivity. Just as employees welcome the comfortably challenging atmosphere of Cisco, so do companies. Cisco's acquisitions work because the acquired companies and employees are able to flourish. The opportunity for growth and success attracts everyone from engineers to millionaire executives.

Cisco has matured and changed as it has grown, punctuated by the transitions in management. Sandy Lerner,

John Morgridge, and John Chambers each are powerful personalities who have left a mark on every aspect of Cisco. Cisco has prospered under the different regimes because of what the three leaders have had in common. The open atmosphere, the frugality, the commitment to customers—all have been preserved over the 15 years of Cisco's existence. Another common thread has been the commitment to extending opportunity. Cisco's charity work is centered around education. The primary thrust there has been to teach people how to build and use networks, which lets them ride the same wave that propels Cisco's success. Cisco has managed to act humble about its success; it listens to its customers, avoids mistakes, and stays excited about the future.

ELECTRONIC HEROIN

In the latter days of 1996, Aurora Phillips, a mild-mannered printed-circuit board (PCB) designer, sat bored at her job at Tandem Computer. The pay was okay, and she worked pretty hard, designing about one board every three months. But something didn't really click. One fateful day she surfed the Web, perhaps searching for meaning in the dense chaos of the Internet. She clicked on a banner ad that was running on various tech-oriented sites at the time, including the Dilbert Zone, the locus for Scott Adams's turnip-shaped, caustic engineer drone. The ad read, "make friends @ Cisco." Cisco's hokey approach to attracting job applicants was markedly different from the formal and aggressive "get a hot job" attitude taken by most in Silicon Valley. Our heroine was whisked to Cisco's Profiler, the company's applicant description form. At the Profiler, she clicked on her job and and answered questions specific to her occupation. The next day, James Rodriguez, a fellow PCB designer, called her at home. He liked what he heard and added his recommendation to her file. A few days later, she made the trip to Tasman Drive, San Jose. Industrial, gray buildings flanked the road for nearly a mile. She met the tall, thin Rodriguez, and hung out with his coworkers, comfortable in the surroundings that soon became hers. In just one week, Phillips had entered the Cisco Zone.

Before she began working at Cisco, Phillips most likely went through Cisco's two-day training program. She wasn't drilled by managers in a coldly lit room; the training program was entirely online and part of Cisco's internal Web site. Signing up with Cisco gave her not just a salary but also a mentor, James Rodriguez. Though he learned about Phillips through Cisco's human resources database, he received Cisco's referral bonus of $1,000 and a Cisco Lotto Card, offering the chance to win Cisco paraphernalia. Because of such incentives and programs, referrals accounted for over 50 percent of Cisco's hires by the time Phillips came on board. Perhaps the most important part of Phillips's employment package was the crucial options plan, commensurate with her position.

The first day began with a tour of the workspace, learning where the coffee and lavatories were. Her cubicle, like the others, faced the outside with sunlight streaming in; executive offices, every one 12 feet square, were built into the middle of the floor. She also received her Cisco worker's badge. It efficiently acted both as a personal identification card and as a pass key to the various Cisco buildings, a common practice in Silicon Valley. On the badge was the phrase "Dedication to Customer Success," put there as a mandate by Chambers to imprint the Cisco values. Once Phillips had her ID card and had filled out the necessary first-day forms, she got to work.

In many of the Cisco departments, the cubicles are run as "nonterritorial offices." Simply put, the cubes are identical and unassigned; each day people sit at any unfilled station. This inevitably leads to a subtle competition for the best spaces. Employees line up outside the door, waiting to get inside, as if for a postholiday sale. Some have found the cube farms understandably disconcerting—not only is the idea of personal space violated, but managers can simply glance at the room to see who the most enthusiastic, early-rising employees are.

As Phillips worked, she didn't need to worry about running errands to the drugstore or the car wash. All material needs were satisfied inside the lettered monoliths. If she needed breakfast, she could go to the company cafeteria as early as 7 A.M. Breakfast time at the cafeteria bettered Starbucks, with steaming espressos and rows of fresh-baked pastries. Lunch (and dinner, as the cafeteria closed at 7 P.M.) could be brick-oven pizza, Asian fusion cuisine, burgers and fries, or a hundred other combinations. Maybe Phillips would need a Cisco T-shirt (though, as with all Silicon Valley companies, free corporate T-shirts were in ample supply). No problem. All and sundry goods could be purchased at McWhorters Express Store in Building J. Money was available from the conveniently located ATM.

Not that she'd have to go down the thickly carpeted stairs or to another building for everything. At the edge of the cubes on Phillips's floor, and in the other alphabetized edifices, stood the break room. Each break room housed one of the fabled refrigerators of many sodas, the free panoply of nonalcoholic beverages that Morgridge once tried—and failed, due to employee discontent—to winnow. The sodas often washed down the endless supply of free popcorn, though employees were encouraged to subsist on something other than the free junk food. If Phillips needed some pants pressed, she would go to the break room. The break room also housed dry-cleaning services, for pick-up and return the next day.

A jaunt from Building A to Building L would provide quite a workout, but not as good as the one she could get at the gym housed in Building L. TimeOut, the Cisco gym, offered Phillips and all the other employees the opportunity to use their bodies instead of their minds, with free weights and StairMasters, aerobics, yoga, tai chi, self-defense classes, and massage. Or she could go outside and play

Chambers's favorite sport on the basketball courts. If Time-Out's health screenings kept her from the doctor, then the monthly dental truck's cleanings could keep her from the dentist. Her car was pampered, too, with onsite washes and oil changes. Cisco provided her all these perks so that she could spend as much time doing her job as possible. That strategy worked with her, as it has with thousands of other Cisco employees. University of California at Santa Barbara Professor of American Culture Chris Newfield described the Cisco life very succinctly: "The corporation is the new public sphere—it's the new neighborhood."[1]

Phillips received her first internal review at the end of her first month. Human Resources gave her a checklist of expected accomplishments and asked her how things were going. Phillips's manager was responsible for handling departmental goals and the work process. Phillips was taught how to develop her own objectives and to understand what her expectations of management at Cisco could be. She then wrote her own objectives to review with her manager, rather than have the manager do it. Barbara Beck, vice president of human resources, explained, "The onus is on the employee. It's a shift of responsibility from the manager to the employee to take more ownership for the job, learning, and career."[2] Phillips also met with John Chambers, a personal touch Chambers extended to all new employees. Three months after being hired, Phillips had already designed five circuit boards. Cisco allowed her to be five times more productive than she had been at Tandem, while paying her in relation to her performance. Cisco also had strong expectations for her. At her second internal review, after six months, she was tested on her understanding of the industry and how her products fit into Cisco's end-to-end solutions.

Cisco's intranet, the Cisco Employee Connection, helped Phillips and the company waste less time on administrivia. The Cisco Employee Connection served the traditional purpose of an intranet, allowing access to common information and news, such as benefits information and corporate announcements. Employees could also tap into searchable corporate databases, including a personnel directory, organizational charts, maps, and phone and e-mail listings. Cisco also added interactive services to the Employee Connection. Phillips could ask Human Resources questions, or report problems with her computer equipment and review the status of fixes.

Phillips and the other engineers in her department spend their days in techie bliss. Though a normal work week is 60 hours, the lack of arbitrarily rigid rules makes the engineers feel proud of their efforts, instead of burdened by stress. Employees are allowed to establish their own flexible work schedules or telecommute (using Cisco products, of course). They get extra-duty pay for working weekends and holidays. When queried by reporters about what it's like to work at Cisco, the response is almost cultish: "It's electronic heroin!" "You're amazed by your own productivity!"[3] "If you are remotely entrepreneurial, you will work crazy hours because you want to, not because you have to."[4] The opportunity to see one's work realized is an especial draw for engineers at Cisco. Cisco's sales and manufacturing capability has been honed over the years to deliver products to consumers as quickly as engineers can design them. Engineers have often welcomed being acquired by Cisco because they know that their work could be realized the instant they have a working product, without any of the difficulties faced by a small company or a less-efficient large company.

Cisco began as a company populated entirely by engineers. Much of its top management is drawn from the ranks of practicing technologists. Each engineering team, whether formed from an acquisition or developed in-house, has retained its own individual atmosphere. The infusion of Cisco values and the strict adherence to workflow standards (exemplified by the standardized IS implemented under Peter Solvik) maintains the coherence necessary in a large company. All units are infused with the

Cisco values, and Cisco stock. The business units and business divisions have remained entrepreneurial throughout their establishment and reorganization, driving to churn out the best product in the shortest amount of time. The pressure is strong and the hours long, but the engineers thrive. For engineers, Cisco works.

Life hasn't necessarily been as much fun for Cisco salespeople. The demands on them have often outpaced the rewards. Perhaps it's Chambers's own sales experience that has caused upper management to push the Cisco sales force so hard. In 1990, as Cisco transformed into a public company under Morgridge's firm hand, there were only about 80 salespeople for the entire country. By 1997, that many people covered a region of a few counties. As territories shrank, so did salaries. Executive salaries in sales were driven down while the top brass, armed with daily sales figures provided on the internal Web site, pushed for better results. Cisco salespeople often had to work longer hours than the work-happy engineers, mirroring Chambers and his 24-hour availability. It took a long time for Cisco to successfully manage the tension between its direct sales staff and its reseller partners.

■ THE MORE THINGS CHANGE...

Cisco's three phases of management are marked by distinct corporate cultures, defined by dominant personalities at the helm. The early years were a reflection of Sandy Lerner and Len Bosack. Len drove himself and the other Cisco employees almost impossibly hard, expecting a commitment of 110 hours a week. Sandy was fanatical about satisfying Cisco's customers. Her frugality and no-holds-barred personality guided Cisco's culture. Both were extremely aggressive in selling their products. They were in the game to win by being the best, the fastest, and the

smartest. Everyone from venture capitalists to other networking companies told them that there was no market
for Cisco's router technology. From the beginning, the
people at Cisco learned to ignore advice that the success of
their products was impossible. They were uninterested in
being bound by traditional strictures of business. This
gave Cisco a free-wheeling, dynamic spirit, but hampered
it in dealings with corporations that prized spit and polish
more than simple efficacy.

Lerner and Bosack went to Don Valentine for corporate know-how, and he brought in John Morgridge. Morgridge, while certainly a suit, enjoyed confrontation and
aggressiveness. Discussions that closely resembled fights
were commonplace. Cisco remained a wild, hairy place to
work. Morgridge provided a constant stream of snappy
comebacks and jocular teasing, but he was a professional.
People began working more reasonable hours, and the
number of employees skyrocketed. Morgridge also shared
the founders' commitment to charity and education.

John Chambers continued the development of Cisco
into a sustainable enterprise. Its culture came to reflect his
attitudes and professed philosophies. He talked fast, but
softly. He was willing to crush the competition, but preferred them to be friends. He flushed out individuals who
disobeyed his vision, but encouraged everyone to voice
their concerns to him. He crowed about Cisco's abilities,
but denigrated his own. He was always available to the customer, except for the times he was utterly committed to his
family. His contradictions led to a management style that
was uniquely flexible yet strong, necessary for the rapidly
evolving and growing Cisco.

Cisco's culture subtly shifted to reflect Chambers's
ideals. The atmosphere became less confrontational and
more professional. A sense of maturity, fostered by Chambers and the company's continuing success, infected
meetings and business dealings. Chambers understood
sales better than any of Cisco's previous leaders, having
worked under the sales machine of IBM. Cisco became a

global company, requiring communication to mitigate misunderstanding.

Chambers extended Cisco's commitment to the customer to the employees, as well. Chambers began meeting the troops at the beginning of his tenure as CEO, and continues to do so though Cisco is now orders of magnitude larger. Employees get to attend special breakfast meetings on their birthdays that allow all members of the Cisco organization to ask Chambers pointed questions about anything concerning the company. Chambers efficiently evokes loyalty in all of Cisco's branches, a loyalty to the idea of a unified company working toward the common purpose of "Dedication to Customer Success."

■ ... THE MORE THEY STAY THE SAME

Though Cisco's culture has developed over the years, what makes it remarkable is its consistency. Though Sandy Lerner and John Chambers have diametrically opposed personalities, the foundations laid by Lerner are still visible under Chambers. Lerner was fanatic about customer service, obsessively frugal, and committedly honest. Morgridge was fanatic about customer service, obsessively frugal, and committedly honest. Chambers is fanatic about customer service, obsessively frugal, and committedly honest. The change in Cisco has been, above all, one of maturation—smooth the founders' rough edges, add years of business experience, and you get Morgridge. Smooth away all the rough edges, and Chambers appears. The founders got it right when they built a company driven to succeed for the customer's sake. Each succeeding generation of management was wise enough not to mess with that plan.

Cisco has tried to make its managers as invisible as possible, the better to make its employees feel like they're in a small, dynamic company. Cisco's culture is cultish in that its process revolves around the expression of shared ideals. By sticking to core values, Cisco has stayed on track while changing tactics, products, and people.

As Cisco grew, it preserved an open atmosphere. Any employee can go into any manager's office, including Chambers's, to talk. Cisco became a federation of entrepreneurial teams, and its culture reflects that. As John Morgridge explained, "We've brought together a lot of cultures. I don't know that an unchanging culture is necessarily optimum." All of Cisco's leaders wanted to avoid creating a rigid culture like that of IBM. For the iconoclastic founders, the idea would have been absurd. Morgridge remembered working with and being pressured by IBM. Chambers knew first hand how stultifying that atmosphere could be. In contrast to the strict hierarchies of traditional corporations, Morgridge asserted, "We are very egalitarian. We have a standard size office; the VPs get a conference room." Moreover, Chambers is a millionaire many times over from his association with Cisco, but so are many other employees; one estimate put 20 percent of Cisco's employees in the millionaire bracket. The Cisco wealth isn't concentrated solely in its management.

People at Cisco can admit to their superiors that they've made a mistake. Janet Skadden was hired in 1994 from Tandem Computers (the same company Aurora Phillips left) to be manager of human resources under Vice President Barbara Beck. Skadden was only six months into her job when she made a serious misstep. She needed to orchestrate a team-building session for 300 Cisco managers. After 13 years at Tandem, Skadden believed that physically engaging activities like trust-falls, where managers fall blindly into each others arms, would work. Though Beck advised her that it might be too "touchy-feely" for Cisco, Skadden went ahead. The results were immediately humbling. As Skadden recalled in a 1997 interview, the managers were saying, "Who thought of this?" "Is this supposed to be fun?" It was a depressing moment for the new hire. But she knew that she could admit failure to her boss. Skadden told Beck that she knew she had screwed up and would take a good look at the corporate culture at Cisco to make sure it wouldn't happen again. In 1997, Beck could barely recall agreeing with Skadden's assessment. Cisco doesn't punish mistakes; it punishes *not learning* from mistakes.[5]

■ THE CORE

Cisco has spread its reach across the globe, but its core—its locus of power—remains on Tasman Drive in San Jose. Cisco's main campus is huge. Employees pedal between the buildings, reminiscent of the bicycle-clogged Stanford campus. Each building looks nearly identical to the next, except for a lettered identification plaque. Starting with Building A, Cisco reached Building O by 1997. The 15 buildings are grouped into Sites 1 through 3. Nearby are 19 numbered buildings at Site 4. Inside this alphabet campus beats the many-chambered heart of the networking giant. Cisco employees happily toil away like robots on Prozac, cocooned by the all-consuming lifestyle, mothered by the beatific John Chambers.

Is the "Cisco way" dangerous? Are its employees losing something by signing on to the Cisco dream? The central campus resembles something like Soviet architecture—bare and faceless on the outside, with dashes of opulence inside to remind all of the power within the walls. Cisco is its own village, and has engendered intense loyalty and happiness through some of the same myth-making techniques used by propagandists. The concept of corporate perks has moved beyond simple fillips to complete need fulfillment. Human Resources maintains lists of Cisco clubs that go way beyond the corporate softball team (and Cisco has several corporate sports teams). Wal-Mart, offering every routine product and service under one roof, has been blamed for destroying small-town life. Cisco, like many other Silicon Valley companies, out-Wal-Marts Wal-Mart. Former employees have commented on the sterility of a life entirely within the Cisco bubble: Nearly everyone there shares same interests, socioeconomic status, and education. Local communities have lost the involvement of the employees of Cisco and other similarly high-commitment companies. And many of those communities are falling apart.

■ GOOD TIMES

People at Cisco are *really* happy. It wasn't a fluke that Aurora Phillips found herself in a happy group of engineers. 3Com founder Bob Metcalfe admiringly admitted, "They have a remarkable knack for keeping good people. I have a number of friends working at Cisco. They're very pleased with Chambers. It's easy to be happy at a company that's winning." Cisco has stayed in a very healthy loop: Being on top makes its employees happy; happy employees keep Cisco on top. "The testimony I get from my friends there is that it's fun. Chambers gives them room to do what they want to do."

In fact, Cisco has given all of its employees, from directly hired managers to acquired engineers, an environment where they can thrive and create new opportunities for themselves. Cisco never lost its entrepreneurial fever. One employee enthused, "Intelligence, learning aptitude, and resourcefulness are more highly prized than the ability to kiss butt."[6] At every turn, ego has been discouraged and productivity rewarded. At Cisco, actions speak better than words. Outsiders often wonder how Cisco has successfully managed the integration of so many different companies. Cisco culture boils down to common sense, in acquired executive Krish Ramakrishnan's opinion. Cisco finds companies that reflect its ideals. It then does as little as possible to change them. "It's all about what's right for your product, and people respect that. We haven't experienced any culture shock. We feel like we've been here since the founding of Cisco."

Cisco has been singularly successful with the employees of companies it acquires. After Cisco had acquired 20 companies, it still employed 10 of their CEOs and 70 percent of their senior management. Annually, Cisco loses only 7 percent of its employees who came from acquired companies, a rate even lower than its overall turnover of 13 percent per year. Admitting his bias, Vice President of Business Development Mike Volpi said in 1997, "I tend to get the impression that we are viewed as a very positive acquirer in that we treat employees very well. We give them excellent opportunities in terms of being able to take the product which they've taken a long time to develop and shoot it out through a distribution channel that can actually carry it." He added that acquired employees appreciate another benefit they receive: "Cisco stock, which I think is considered a very good currency." Cisco's professed strategy to acquire only companies with top-notch potential worked for it, as well. Each new acquisition's employees knew that Cisco's management considered their product and strategy to be crucial to Cisco's future success. In July 1997, when Cisco acquired Dagaz, the xDSL component of Integrated Network Corporation, the Dagaz employees gave Volpi, the architect of the acquisition, a standing ovation. In Volpi's words, "I'd say that's pretty positive."[7]

Volpi believes that engineering and marketing are the creative engine, which is why Cisco keeps those teams fairly independent and intact. Cisco takes a long time to choose its acquisitions, and then protects their people. Acquired employees continue to report to their former CEO, who becomes a VP reporting to the line-of-business head. To Volpi, the management team is one of the key assets. He asserted that the hardest talent to find is senior management, more so than even good engineering. As he said, "All these start-ups are run by very smart people." Like Barbara Beck and John Chambers, Mike Volpi knows that he's responsible for acquiring people who may be smarter than he is himself. This humility in managers, while often professed, seems real at Cisco.

Krish Ramakrishnan's company, Internet Junction, was acquired in 1995. He welcomed the opportunity Cisco offered. "What technologists like to see is the success of their product; that sometimes overrides the glory angle of taking it public. We jumped on the Cisco bandwagon because it was great for our product." He was in charge of his destiny 3 years later, with a group of 20 people. He didn't feel any different, because his team was still making entrepreneurial decisions. "Within Cisco there are pockets of entrepreneurial growth." Cisco has relied on these pockets to survive, for no networking company can succeed without the ability to continuously grow. It allowed friendly competition between different units to persist. Ramakrishnan felt that Cisco isn't a monolithic company, because there are lots of small groups, each trying to make its product a success.

The entrepreneurial spirit didn't reach every employee. As Ramakrishnan said, growth exists in pockets. One employee stated in a 1997 interview, "I'd never work for a company as large as Cisco again, because getting anything done is like being in a vat of molasses. You can't really be creative around here and have it work with any kind of time frame." Stephanie Hafner was fed up with the unavoidable bureaucracy that appeared even at Cisco, a company that prided itself on its commitment to productivity. "You have to go through a million people to get anything done."[8] Cisco is not a small, entrepreneurial company, however hard it tries to preserve that culture.

■ MONEY MATTERS

Cisco's transition from start-up to enterprise was finalized when founders Lerner and Bosack sold their 67 percent stake in Cisco back to the company after leaving in 1990. That act has greatly abetted the company's success. Cisco immediately had vast reserves of assets available to acquire people and companies. It certainly would have been more difficult for the board to give Morgridge and Chambers the same stock rewards without the founders' share. Cisco encourages its employees to own Cisco stock. The human resources department touts the Cisco stock purchase plan: Each year $25,000 in Cisco stock can be purchased by an employee at 85 percent of the opening or closing price of the previous 6 months, whichever is lower. Combined with the stock options given to employees as part of their employment packages—a senior engineer might be given nearly a year's salary in options—the purchase plan has given nonexecutive employees over 40 percent of stock held by Cisco insiders.

The stock options have caused some problems with Cisco's employees. Due to the stock's meteoric rise, employees hired at different times could have similar stock option packages with wildly different values. As Beck explained in 1998, "The value of the stock is quite different today than three years ago. Due to seniority, there are employees with different stock values doing the same jobs." The strength of the stock allowed Cisco to be lax in offering competitive salaries. One of the founding engineers had a salary of only $25,000, way below market average, when Cisco went public in 1990. He became rich on Cisco stock, not salary. Over the years, Cisco has stairstepped and gone up in salaries and bonuses and down on options to be more reflective of the market.

Cisco has come closer to the market average, but still lags. Pay causes some employee dissatisfaction, if only for the simple reason that Silicon Valley is overpriced and oversaturated with money. One complained, "The pay scales definitely need adjustment to reflect the extremely high cost of living, as well as the fact that most people in my department are recent college grads with big loans."[9] However, the cachet of working at Cisco can translate to a

60 percent higher salary at another company. Even so, annual turnover remains lower than the industry average. Even if the pay might be better elsewhere, Cisco wins by being one of the best places to work.

Bonuses driven by Cisco's year-after-year success became, next to direct stock options, one of Cisco's most powerful tools to drive "customer success." The large annual bonuses reward both corporate success and customer happiness. Cisco has always prided itself on high customer satisfaction. In 1994, Cisco's customer satisfaction survey showed that about 65 percent of its customers were completely happy with their treatment by Cisco. That year, Morgridge and Chambers tied one-third of the yearly bonus for most of the company's employees to the customer satisfaction survey. The next year, satisfaction rose to about 85 percent, and stayed there. In fact, bonuses have come to dominate managerial salaries. The year-end bonuses, in large part tied to customer satisfaction, gave directors 85 percent of their salary in 1996, for example.

Small bonuses that reward success are also common. Anyone can give immediate bonuses of up to $2,000 in value to a fellow employee for superlative work, with approval from the appropriate superior. In May 1999, Cisco extended its bonus system by signing up with Netcentives. Netcentives was a San Francisco company that began by marketing ClickRewards, an incentives program designed for Web portals to encourage repeat business. Netcentives began using ClickRewards to entice new hires, and recognized its potential for human resource departments. It reconfigured the program and sold it to Cisco and other companies, including Microsoft, as an employee-bonus program. Cisco primarily used the program for its customer service representatives. The reps earned bonus points—from 50 points for encouraging customers to use Cisco's online demonstrations, up to 1,500 points for meeting monthly online sales quotas. The points were convertible directly into frequent-flier miles, or redeemable for anything from a music CD (900 points) to a Cisco-emblazoned leather bomber jacket trimmed in wool (20,000 points).[10]

■ HOW TO INFLUENCE PEOPLE

Barbara Beck has one of the hardest jobs at Cisco. All she's had to do as vice president of human resources for the last 10 years is hire about 1,000 new employees each quarter.

At any time, Cisco has hundreds of openings. Beck has used any tactic to attract applicants, including the Friends campaign that brought in Aurora Phillips. In 1997, Cisco tweaked its Web server to target its competition. According to Beck, Cisco watched for people coming from one of its competitors to its home page. Cisco routed those people from the normal "Welcome to Cisco" page to a "Welcome to Cisco, would you like a job?" site. Beck explained, "If someone was aggressive enough to try to check up on their competitor, we figured we could use that person."[11]

Referrals remain Cisco's primary means of finding new hires. Barbara Beck updated the Friends campaign with a push to get "Amazing People" referrals. The employee who made the most referrals would get a one-year lease on a Porsche Boxster, a little better reward than a Cisco travel mug. From the management perspective, Cisco won as well, as the in-house campaign brought in more hires than outside advertising would have. Not only that, but the Boxster lease cost less than a half-page advertisement in Silicon Valley's number-one rag, the San Jose *Mercury News*. Cisco's outside recruiting was also nontraditional. Over the summer of 1999, Cisco crewed booths at local arts festivals, such as the Afribbean Music and Cultural Festival and the Los Altos Arts and Wine Festival, and put up ads at movie houses showing *Star Wars Episode I: The Phantom Menace*.

Of course, Beck also handles firing employees. Cisco's culture isn't for everyone. Chambers is unforgiving of people who can't agree with his corporate vision. However, the firm's process is made as equitable as possible. Beck discussed how Cisco handles breaking up with an employee. "When someone doesn't work out, it's one of the hardest things we do." Cisco's no-fault separation policy is in marked contrast to policies at many other places that assign employees to a performance improvement plan. Those who don't reach the given milestones are terminated. Cisco, emulating Chambers's constant desire for self-improvement, tries to come to a solution that is agreed to by both parties. At the second internal review, the milestones designed by the employee are reviewed, and if the employee has not met them or is unhappy with Cisco, he or she is given the opportunity to accept the no-fault separation. This severance package is designed to allow employees "to leave feeling good about the company and with their respect and dignity intact,"[12] Beck explained. If an employee comes to her and says that it isn't working out, Cisco provides a severance policy as long as the departure is mutually agreed to. Where there is still hope, Cisco works with the employee to change the situation for the better, offering counseling options and a performance improvement plan. According to Beck, turnover is 13 percent, mostly by mutual agreement. Because of Cisco's commitment to fairness, disgruntled ex-Cisco employees are almost as hard to find as dissatisfied current employees.

The human resources department is also responsible for developing the skills of its employees. Human Resources uses employees' self-developed goals as a guide. It also runs a variety of training programs, including some for potential recruits. Cisco offers a 10-week internship to business school students in the hope that they'll stick with the company. The MBAs hone their abilities in market research and financial analysis, working toward a summary strategic business plan relevant to a networking segment company.

■ BUILDING FOR THE FUTURE

Cisco's training extends outside its walls, fitting the Cisco ideal of the networked business. Cisco has programs designed to train industry professionals in the use of Cisco products. It looked to the future when it established the Cisco Networking Academy for high school and college students. Cisco's programs have grown exponentially in the years since their introduction. The Cisco Certified Internetworking Expert (CCIE) program began in 1993. By 1999, the training program had grown to become the Cisco Career Certifications program, available around the globe, with multiple certification levels in both network support and design, covering routing and switching, dial-up, SNA, and wide-area networks. The Networking Academy began in October 1997 with a partnership with one school. By the end of 1998, over 1,000 students had entered one of the 582 Networking Academies in 43 states and 8 other countries. As 1999 neared its close, the Networking Academy program had established a presence in all 50 states and 49 countries outside the United States.

The Cisco Networking Academy was an initiative that combined an online curriculum with hands-on networking labs. It gave high schools, colleges, and nonprofit educational organizations the opportunity to offer students a class on the basics of networking science, using cutting-edge technology and hands-on learning to teach vocational skills necessary for jobs in the quickly growing, high-paying IT industry. Training was free, and the multimedia curriculum almost ran itself on an NT server donated by Microsoft. The 20 to 35 students in each class actually built networks (with a minimum of five routers and two switches) using the equipment owned by the school. Schools looking to help their students catch the Internet wave enthusiastically welcomed the Cisco Networking Academy. The success of the program came as no surprise to Cisco.

The program soon developed a hierarchical structure that allowed for its rapid deployment. On the front lines, a school designated as a local academy would teach the curriculum to students. Students who completed the sequence would take an online test to be certified as Cisco Network Associates. The instructors at the local academies were themselves taught by a regional academy, most often a college. Each regional academy would usually support at least 10 local academies. Regional academies designated as Cisco Academy Training Centers could train instructors at other regional academies. Finally, the training center instructors would be trained directly by Cisco. Because the curriculum and training procedures had been rigidly defined, Cisco could stay many levels away from the front-line classrooms without fear that the program would be mistaught.

Cisco certainly does well with the program. Cisco employees only have to train the training center instructors. The curriculum is entirely owned by Cisco and cannot be used outside of the Cisco Networking Academy program. The equipment for the lab must be from Cisco. A Cisco technical support package has to be purchased yearly after the first year an academy signs on. Finally, the program produces *Cisco* Network Associates, trained on Cisco products with a Cisco curriculum. The Networking Academy offers students a hybrid of a solid education in the theoretical foundations underlying networking and corporate training in the Cisco product line. Robert X. Cringely apologetically compared the Networking Academy's strange mix of philanthropy and propaganda to the Hitler Youth in a June 1999 column.[13]

Network associates can go on to the higher levels of certification that are available to industry professionals. In fact, the only requirement for certification as a Cisco Network Associate is success on a certification exam. Cisco's training partners offer a variety of intensive (and expensive) courses to prepare students for the exams. The corporate training consists of blitzkrieg lectures that discuss how to use Cisco products, very unlike the gradual and generally hands-on education offered by the Networking Academies. Cisco is continually making changes to the certification program, adding new certifications and modifying old ones as new products, technologies, and networking models are introduced. In 1999, Cisco had two main lines of certification for a number of networking technologies, in network support and network design.

The holy grail of Cisco training is the Cisco Certified Internetworking Expert examination. Originally offered for Cisco's routing and switching products in 1993, there were also WAN switching (the StrataCom line), ISP/dial-up, and SNA/IP certifications by 1999. To become a CCIE, applicants must pass a rigorous exam and then survive a two-day laboratory exam at one of nine global facilities. In the grueling two-day laboratory test, applicants for the different CCIE areas must build and configure a complex network of the appropriate kind from scratch. The creation of certification levels was welcomed by many in the support business, as the CCIE certification process is grueling and expensive.

Cisco has begun the process of developing a charitable arm. The Virtual Schoolhouse Grant program to enable school networking was established in 1996. Only in 1997 was the general Cisco Foundation established. The 1998 brochure described the Cisco Foundation's goal as funding "programs that help people become self-sufficient and productive individuals." These programs ranged from those providing the basic necessities, such as shelters and soup kitchens, to long-term health care and education organizations. The donation amounts in 1998, for a $100 billion company, weren't staggering. The most money, $6 million, was spent on the Ciscocentric Networking Academies. Employees gave $345,000 (or about three senior engineers' salaries) in matching gifts, $90,000 in charitable payroll deductions, and $75,000 worth of equipment (which, with employee discounts, cost them $20,000 or less). The Cisco Foundation directed its money into the communities near its facilities. In 1999, organizations within 50 miles of San Jose, Chelmsford, Research Triangle Park, and New York City could apply for community grants.

In 1999, Chambers unveiled a much more ambitious project, NetAid. Working with the U.N. Development Program, Cisco brought the idea behind the "We Are the World" concert to the Internet age. NetAid began as three concerts simultaneously broadcast from New York, London, and Paris on October 6—with somewhat incongruous elements, such as a duet between Wyclef Jean and U2's Bono in Giants Stadium. The resulting radio broadcast reached the largest audience in history. The legacy of the concert was the NetAid Web site, meant as an online clearing ground for making charitable donations and volunteering to combat hunger, environmental degradation, or other global problems. Each page, of course, prominently displays the Cisco logo. Cisco reported an $8 million donation to the NetAid project, with another $2 million in a matching challenge grant with its employees.

By comparison, Sandy Lerner and Len Bosack have given about $120 million to nonprofit organizations and research through the Leonard K. Bosack and Bette M. Kruger Foundation. As Sandy told a *Wired* reporter in November 1999, "It's an embarrassment that people in Silicon Valley are giving so little."[14]

■ MODEL OF SUCCESS

Cisco soon cashed in on its success and started selling answers. Just as customers convinced Cisco to first move into switching, and then into end-to-end solutions, they began clamoring for Cisco to provide consulting services. Chambers sold Cisco as a model of how to organize and run a company. In 1997, Cisco pushed telecommuting and the Global Networked Business model based on Peter Solvik's

IT initiatives. Cisco's press releases crowed that the model "is now in the Smithsonian Institution's permanent research collection" because it was a finalist in a Smithsonian awards competition. The premier 1998 strategy at Cisco was "multiservice networking," another phrase to describe data and voice convergence.

At the end of 1998, Cisco established the Internet Business Solutions Group to work with consulting companies such as Cambridge Technology Partners, Ernst & Young, and KPMG to advise businesses on how to deploy Internet-powered solutions. The VP of the group, Sue Bostrom, asserted in the buzzword-laden press release, "Cisco is a great example of an Internet-based company." 1999 saw the introduction of the Workforce Optimization solution, yet another networking consultancy initiative. Later that year, Cisco purchased a 20 percent stake in KPMG, the consulting firm that had helped Cisco establish its intranet in 1993. Chambers wants to lead Cisco by following his customers' needs, but his customers are asking Cisco to guide them. Cisco is just entering an era in which it will play the role of senior statesman in an industry that drives the economy. Though the potential rewards are great, so are the dangers.

Chapter

Routing the Industry (1997–1998)

■ THE NIA THREAT ■ STICKS AND STONES
■ PARTNERSHIPS AND ALLIANCES
■ SWITCHING FAST ■ AN IMPLICIT VICTORY

By 1997, Cisco sales reps had breezily usurped and adapted IBM's old mantra. "You can't get fired for purchasing our internetworking gear," they boasted. And it was true. Cisco had established itself as the gold standard in networking gear. Since Chambers first assumed the title of CEO, Cisco's market capitalization had skyrocketed from $4 billion to more than $43 billion. Just as Microsoft had gained dominance in the software industry, Intel had won control of the semiconductor world, and IBM had once dominated the computer business, Cisco had proved its sovereignty over the networking universe. Like Intel's "Intel Inside" promotions, Cisco was cultivating its brand with "Cisco-Powered Networks," convincing network providers to advertise the fact that they used Cisco equipment. In an understatement, Chambers told *Network World* that year, "I think we have a chance to shape the future of the industry."[1]

Key to this success was an emphatic technological agnosticism. Such open-mindedness translated directly into a readiness to adopt emerging technologies. Such versatility enabled Cisco to provide the range of hardware and software components necessary to build a desktop-to-desktop product line. Such depth and breadth translated into Cisco's predominance as a one-stop provider of networking equipment.

As Cisco became more and more powerful, its biggest competitors—3Com, Bay Networks, and IBM—became increasingly threatened. So did its smaller competitors, like Xylan and Interphase. After all, they feared losing their customers if Cisco developed a near-monopoly of Microsoft proportion. Myriad questions about Cisco accompanied its role as market mover: What impact would Cisco have on its competition? What impact would its dominance have on Internet technology? What made Cisco any different from a Microsoft of networking? How could Cisco remain the market leader and benefit symbiotically from emerging technologies that its competition provided?

■ THE NIA THREAT

The Networking Interoperability Alliance (NIA), founded by IBM, Bay Networks, and 3Com soon after Cisco's StrataCom acquisition in 1996, continued to clamor for alliances against Cisco. The idea was to create a band of "littler people"—Davids against Cisco's Goliath, in their eyes—to help customers simplify, standardize, and enhance the design and deployment of networks composed of multiple brands of products. As in the PC business, the founders figured, decoupling hardware and software would enable the networking industry to grow rapidly at the expense of vertically integrated behemoths like Cisco.

In addition to the three core founding companies, the NIA also included endorsing members such as Xylan, General Datacom Corporation, and First Virtual Corporation. The NIA strategy was to test a variety of products from different companies (including Cisco) to determine which would work well with one another. Vehemently opposed to Cisco's one-stop shopping concept, their idea was to give customers a means to economically and intelligently pick and choose from the best of all manufacturers' products. Clients could then grow hybrid networks with assurance.

The NIA sponsored testing at the University of New Hampshire's InterOperability Laboratory (IOL) to identify and correct interoperability problems in its members' products. In 1997, they opened interoperability tests to nonmember vendors, allowing all networking producers in the industry (including Cisco) to come to New Hampshire to test the compatibility of their equipment. Independently monitored by the Tolly Group, a technology consulting firm, at midyear the tests focused on interoperability using ATM. They ran a live video collaboration application running on equipment from NIA founders 3Com, IBM, and Bay, as well as equipment from other participants, such as First Virtual, GDC, FVC, Interphase, Xylan, FORE, and Olicom. Other tests involved equipment from US Robotics, Xylan, and Madge. Although Cisco was invited to participate in the testing, it declined. Members provided Cisco routers for comprehensive interoperability testing.

NIA promised to work symbiotically on a multivendor standard in four distinct areas: desktops and servers, edge networking, core networking, and network management. For example, the NIA would develop more intelligent systems for desktops and servers by gracing switches and other devices with special capabilities, such as quality-of-service (QoS) and network management features. The NIA's goal was to support existing standards and to monitor each other's products by promoting the development and standardization of new features and functions.

At the end of the tests, the NIA published a "cookbook" specifying how devices from the participating companies could be configured to provide an efficient multivendor network. Their recipe, essentially, was to create an alternative standard that would blunt the influence of Cisco's own Internetwork Operating System (IOS). The NIA was critical to the further success of 3Com, Bay, and IBM and represented a significant effort against a perceived juggernaut. It also posed an explicit challenge for Cisco: The networking giant would have to be more nimble than the Davids.

■ STICKS AND STONES

The NIA posed a small threat, but not one unusual or insurmountable to a company of Cisco's size. The usual challenges of being the market leader galvanized Cisco to make several strategic moves to maintain its status in 1997. The company had to work hard to continue to keep its customers' loyalty, maintain its technological cutting edge, promote its brand name, be aggressively cost competitive, and cultivate and maintain alliances. In 1997, Cisco made several strategic moves to maintain its dominion.

➤ Boosting the Brand

Cisco decided to launch a critical branding campaign in June 1997, promoting "Cisco-Powered Networks." The crusade debuted with full-page ads gracing the *Wall Street Journal* and London's *Financial Times*. The campaign strategically began on the same day as Cisco-sponsored executive service provider forums in Washington and London. Along with the slogan, the campaign boosted the corporate branding strategy of the Cisco name and bridge logo.

The campaign particularly targeted resellers and service providers that sold networks with Cisco equipment, rather than companies installing networks in their own offices. Customers with networks made up of at least 75 percent Cisco parts (depending upon the product line) could apply for kits with an application to acquire rights to use the Cisco-Powered Network logo in advertising, marketing, and collateral materials. Participants had other requirements, as well: They had to maintain a certain high standard of network quality and purchase at least $4 million of infrastructure equipment per year. British Telecom, @Home, CompuServe, and Digex immediately signed up for the program. Lesser-known service carriers—Digex, for example—that used 100 percent Cisco gear in their networks could advertise their own names in league with that of the premier worldwide networking provider. Cisco also announced plans to support its campaign partners with higher levels of marketing and program support on the Cisco Connection Web site.

The Cisco campaign benefited Cisco by maintaining high standards and sales among participants and, more important, by strengthening ties with its customers, boosting brand-name equity, and drawing attention to the often-overlooked parts that constitute networks. The Cisco-Powered Networks campaign was Cisco's first foray into the sphere of the home networking market. Like the long-range recognition of the Intel Inside logo, Cisco's hope was that consumers would likewise recognize the Cisco name and equate it with quality and dependability. The consumer market was nascent; Cisco still hadn't even produced a television commercial. But brand recognition would be a beneficial investment in the future.

➤ Aggressively Licensing the IOS

Along with the Cisco-Powered Networks campaign, Cisco also began to assert branding for its Internetwork Operating System (IOS). Since the days of Lerner, Bosack, Yeager, and Lougheed, Cisco's software had evolved to become the core of the company. The IOS began as an abstract concept to describe the various network services that Cisco's source code handled, including routing protocols. For many years, the IOS was more a marketing tool than an actual integrated software system, but by 1997 it had become the unifying foundation of the product lines—the sum and substance that pervaded most Cisco products and ensured their compatibility with other Cisco parts. This increasingly powerful IOS was one reason why the NIA had banded together. Bits and pieces of the IOS ran through and connected Cisco technology, from standalone routers to hubs, switches, PC and workstation file servers, and other devices. One of the first things Cisco did with technology from acquisitions—StrataCom's switches, for example—was to add IOS code to its platform so that it could work with Cisco's existing product line. The value of common networking code is clear. If Cisco products didn't work well together, Cisco's competitors would have no reason to fear Cisco as a one-stop vendor. Cisco's strength as it expanded into new product areas was its adhesion—and the IOS was the glue.

Chambers shifted customers' attention toward the *code* that made the Cisco system work. All routers and switches run on proprietary software—code—that enables them to talk to one another. As technology evolves, so does the code. In fact, Cisco's view is that the software has the potential to surpass the hardware, even to make it possible to "upgrade" equipment by just adding new and more versatile software.

Each Cisco product has its own relevant IOS code installed. Any non-Cisco product could, with some tailoring, also run on the Cisco IOS. This arrangement was particularly desirable in the case of potential acquisitions—companies with equipment already running on the IOS would be that much easier to integrate into Cisco's product line. Just as Microsoft licensed its Windows operating system to PC manufacturers, Cisco had been licensing its IOS to other networking equipment manufacturers. Over time, it became apparent that software licensing could work strongly in Cisco's favor. Just as Windows became the standard desktop operating system for PCs, it was Cisco's hope that the IOS would become the standard for the entire networking industry. The strategy was well planned: Cisco's IOS would become a brand name among experts in the industry. Even its competitors would seem to adopt it—although perhaps as an unenthusiastic admission that their systems would have to be Cisco-compatible in order to be more saleable. If customers didn't purchase all their hardware directly from Cisco, they still would essentially be buying Cisco code. Cisco would then win even if customers didn't buy Cisco equipment. All licensees would be contractually prohibited from modifying the software in any way.

In 1997, IOS licensees included significant entities such as Compaq, Hewlett-Packard, Cabletron, Digital Equipment Corporation, NEC, Ungermann-Bass, LanOptics, Lannet, and Optical Data Systems. Microsoft and Intel likewise signed up for licenses. Companies leveraging the Cisco IOS software technology in WAN-based products included Alcatel, Ericsson, GTE Government Systems, Northern Telecom, SCITEC, and US Robotics. In an ironic twist, Cisco also licensed the IOS to competitors Bay Networks and 3Com indirectly—the NIA founders had acquired companies that had previously adopted IOS technology.

➤ Slashing Prices

Cisco's dominance gave it another huge advantage. It sold so much gear, it could slash prices dramatically. At the end of 1996, Cisco slashed the price of its networking switches by half, undercutting Bay Network's switch by roughly 50 percent. The Bay switch was more expensive to produce. Competitors could not compete with Cisco's volume pricing. But they were forced to cut prices in order to remain competitive, and prices dropped precipitously. The price war at the beginning of 1997 hurt small competitors as well, including Xylan, whose stock plummeted as a result of Wall Street skepticism about its fourth-quarter earnings.

➤ Focusing on the Small Players

Although he claimed to be paranoid, Chambers wasn't as concerned about competition coming from other giants, like Bay or IBM, as he was about the smaller players, like Ascend, FORE, and Cascade. FORE, Chambers maintained, was Cisco's greatest competitor in the workgroup and ATM areas, and Cascade was its main threat in WAN switching. He was more worried about small players in niche markets that could eat away at pieces of Cisco's business.

Watching out for the small players was one of the early lessons Chambers learned from studying Hewlett-Packard's tactics. The HP model, Chambers maintained, breaks its market down into segments. As a result, Chambers didn't regard Cisco's market as one internetworking marketplace, but, rather as a consortium of smaller markets such as LAN switching, WAN switching, workgroup switching, and access. Cisco's competitors in each of these segments were different from one another.

The telecom industry became a market for Cisco as the data giant began realizing the big bucks involved in sending voice over the Internet. Little Juniper Networks, in this regard, emerged as a quickly moving presence on Cisco's radar. One year old in 1997, the start-up was warming up to release products that were 100 times faster than Cisco's, prompting Cisco's larger competitors, like 3Com and Lucent, to invest in it. Juniper, founded by engineers from Sun, MCI, and Cisco itself, announced that its chips were designed specifically for Internet traffic through phone switches.

The smaller, more agile, companies tend to be the ones with the most innovative technology. Other networking start-ups that branched into the telecom industry included Pluris, Avici, and Torrent Networking. Keeping abreast of their developments, Chambers keeps a closely guarded list of all the small rivals in all the various factions of the networking industry. He tracks them regularly, he says, as a defensive measure and in order to develop Cisco's ongoing strategies in engineering and acquisitions.

➤ Cultivating a Virtual Culture

Just as the popularity of *Star Trek* precipitated a clan of Klingon-speaking fans, the proliferation of the IOS caused a similar fallout in the Cisco world. The Cisco NetWorkers conferences, like science fiction conventions, became inundated with network engineers speaking in foreign, proprietary tongues. Newsgroups and special-interest listservs on the Web teem with Cisco users speaking "Cisco." Cisco essentially created its own language. Nouns and verbs in Cisco-speak include AccessPath, ClickStart, Control-Stream, Fast Step, FragmentFree, JumpStart, Kernel Proxy, LAN2LAN Enterprise and Remote Office, MGX, MICA, Natural Network Viewer, NetSonar, Point and Click Internetworking, RouteStream, Secure Script, SMARTnet, StreamView, SwitchProbe, TrafficDirector, TransPath, VirtualStream, EtherChannel, and FastHub.

As the Web grew, so did the Cisco Connection Online (CCO) Web site, launched in 1996, which facilitated the congregation of Cisco customers. It grew exponentially, boasting 150,000 active registered users from around the world by 1997. In its annual report that year, Cisco announced that the CCO was accessed approximately 1.5 million times each month, enabling customers to learn about new Cisco products, ask and answer questions, and converse with customer and technical support when necessary. For international customers, portions of the CCO were translated into multiple languages, with pages for nearly 50 countries. Over 70 percent of Cisco's technical support for customers and resellers was delivered over the Web, saving Cisco money and, moreover, creating and maintaining a cohesive community.

In the spring of 1997, Cisco Chief Information Officer Peter Solvik, who had taken over the management of the Web site, negotiated an arrangement with My Yahoo! to provide a Cisco version of the popular customized page, allowing Cisco employees to track breaking news reports, competitor activities, general high-tech industry news, and current data on the financial markets.

By effectively cultivating a unique community and language associated with its products, Cisco created an intangible barrier against competitors. Keeping close to the customer through culture, from Sandy Lerner's customer advocacy group onward, became part of the Cisco way.

■ PARTNERSHIPS AND ALLIANCES

Even with its acquisition strategy, Cisco executives know from its early days that they could not do everything. Morgridge, therefore, started a strategy of forming alliances with companies that had complementary products, if buying the companies outright would take Cisco too far from its core competencies. The 1993 business plan made forming strategic alliances one of Cisco's top four goals. As Don Valentine explained, "We made a matrix of the products we needed. We needed resources and we couldn't hire all the talent we needed. I encouraged making investments in venture-sized companies." Morgridge had already been forming alliances to extend Cisco's reach without diluting its focus. Chambers has asserted that Cisco learned early on that it was better to form partnerships and share revenues than to do everything itself.

Cisco, from the outset, formed alliances with industry giants to quickly gain a global presence. Its routers had been instrumental in the global expansion of the Internet; some of its first routers were sold to bring Europe into the National Science Foundation net (NSFNet). The entire world wanted Cisco's routers, but Cisco lacked the necessary worldwide sales and service presence. So, it began cutting deals—by 1994, 13 major Japanese firms, including NEC, Softbank, Hitachi, and Fujitsu, had invested $40 million in Cisco's Japanese subsidiary, Nihon Cisco. The joint venture was strategically timed to take advantage of the still-embryonic Japanese internetworking market. Unsurprisingly, Japan became Cisco's fastest-growing market. A year later, Cisco enjoyed a 60 percent market share in each of its business segments, one of the few foreign companies to succeed on Japanese soil. Other deals with global companies, including Hewlett-Packard and IBM, gave Cisco worldwide service capabilities. Multibillion-dollar companies gave Cisco footholds that it used, as it grew, to dominate global data communications. Strategic alliances became one of Cisco's top priorities as the company grew.

Chambers's rules for a strategic alliance were threefold:

1. It has to benefit the customers. The alliance needs to make sense to the customers. They need to understand the goals of the alliance.
2. It has to result, within 3 years, in $500 million to $1 billion in incremental revenue per year.
3. It needs to be a competitive landscape change for both partners.

Chambers was able to choose alliances that were potentially earthshaking. Anything less would be an insult to the might and vision of Cisco. Alliances under Chambers's reign were dramatically different from those of the early days of Cisco's growth. Each year under his leadership, he made an alliance with a different, larger entity until, by 1997, the need for big alliances diminished as Cisco gained more and more of its own momentum, often cornering a market. Cisco now uses alliances more to manage its potential competition, rather than to bully it. While Microsoft was known for forming alliances in order to learn a partner's business and take it over entirely, Cisco's approach was to manage the relationship for as long as possible.

➤ Hubs

In the years before it went on its acquisition spree, the first alliances Cisco fashioned were with various makers of hubs—devices that retransmit an incoming signal without analysis or redirection. Cisco historically attempted these alliances in order to combine the capabilities of its routers with those of the other-brand hubs. In May 1992, Cisco and Digital joined to add low-cost workgroup routing modules to Digital's DEChubs. CEO Morgridge attempted a more far-reaching alliance with leading hub maker SynOptics in the autumn of 1992. Its goal was the goofily named Rub System. By April 1993, Cisco and SynOptics put out press releases announcing a "shift in the Rub System effort." The shift was, in effect, to give up. Cisco and SynOptics had divergent ideas about what networks should be. Though their products did not compete directly with each other, Cisco promoted router-based networks while SynOptics promoted hub-based networks. The differences were too great, and the technical challenges too unwieldy. The industry would continue to debate the merits and disadvantages of integrating hubs and routers for years.

The lesson from the failed SynOptics partnership was that Cisco would benefit more by entering partnerships with companies that were not direct competitors. Never again in its history of alliances would Cisco partner with a company that was a head-on competitor.

In 1994, Cisco partnered with as many hub makers as it could. Morgridge and Chambers saw that a tight engineering relationship with a top player like SynOptics hadn't worked out, so they established simpler relationships with the entire field. Cisco supplied the technology that allowed companies such as Cabletron, LanOptics, Digital, Optical Data Systems, and Chipcom to add Cisco router modules to their hubs. Hub maker UB Networks was especially entwined with Cisco; in an October 17 agreement, UB Networks began reselling Cisco products, and integrated Cisco router hardware and software into its own products. In these cases, Cisco's partnerships were beneficial to other companies while ensuring that its own market share would grow.

➤ Hewlett-Packard

The next big alliance Morgridge made was with an indirect competitor, Hewlett-Packard—perhaps Cisco's most successful alliance ever. Morgridge and Chambers always had great respect for the computing giant and its CEO, Lew Platt. After all, Hewlett-Packard was the seminal Stanford start-up, inspiring generations of Stanford University students to build their own companies. The other Cisco executives saw its dynamic flexibility as a model for Cisco. It was only appropriate that Cisco would partner aggressively with Hewlett-Packard.

In September 1994, Cisco joined Hewlett-Packard in a far-ranging alliance. Hewlett-Packard, like other hub makers, would incorporate Cisco router modules in its Advance-Stack hub line. Moreover, the two companies agreed to merge their ATM and LAN switching programs in an attempt to catch up to the front-runners. FORE Systems had been first out of the gate with ATM switches in 1992; it and other new companies were growing rapidly. Networking companies were furiously competing to develop the high-speed successor to the Ethernet LAN, called VGAnyLAN. Under the terms of the alliance, Cisco agreed to nonexclusively incorporate Hewlett-Packard's LAN technology, which was also being promoted by AT&T and IBM.

Hewlett-Packard strengthened its ties to Cisco in 1995, becoming the first Cisco partner to be both a reseller and a service provider. Cisco trained Hewlett-Packard's technical support teams, which allowed Cisco to offer worldwide 24-hour customer service. Hewlett-Packard then provided complete networking services, able to sell and support every component, from servers to routers.

In the years that have followed, the Hewlett-Packard–Cisco alliance has continued to be productive, uniquely uniting Cisco's computing and networking strengths with Hewlett-Packard's Unix and Windows capabilities in order to harness the Internet to deliver options to telecom service providers, big corporations, and consumers. John Chambers and Lew Platt are also good buddies now, always seen joking with each other at conferences.

➤ IBM

Cisco's third big alliance, with IBM, was more complex than the previous ones. Chambers and Morgridge admired IBM's computing division of the 1950s and 1960s. Cisco's customers came to them looking for a complete networking solution, like IBM's old total computing package. However, Chambers had experienced the crumbling of IBM's power first hand, watching it fail to move effectively from mainframes to minicomputers when he worked there in sales. Beginning in 1992, IBM had abandoned its own networking products for those of other companies (some of which it acquired): Lotus, Tivoli, 3Com, Proteon, Bay Networks, Cisco, Xylan, and Cascade. This mishmash of products lost IBM its traditional ace in the hole: authoritative credibility. Even though mainframe networking was a growing market, IBM's networking division, whose top people had fled for greener pastures, was looking more and more like the lifeless Sahara.

Nevertheless, Morgridge and Chambers wanted the alliance with IBM because there were a lot of IBM mainframes out there that needed networking, while IBM's networking group was falling apart. The first attempts to form an alliance with Big Blue failed. Don Valentine described the first time Cisco approached IBM for a partnership. "We attempted to work with IBM. Ellen Hancock was in charge of networking and she wouldn't even see us. We volunteered to fly to London to meet with her when she was there, and she finally met us. She bluntly said that Microsoft had taken advantage of IBM in the PC business and it would never happen again: Cisco was the enemy."

IBM had strong reasons to distrust networking alliances due to its involvement in the 3Com-Microsoft fiasco (as described in Chapter 2). But it was even more foolish not to ally with Cisco. As Valentine explained, "Ellen [Hancock] and IBM wanted to sustain SNA [Systems Networking Architecture, IBM's proprietary networking protocol] as the networking standard, and we were willing to work with that. Since they wouldn't work with us, however, we decided to dismantle SNA. That made life simpler for us at Cisco, but it would have benefited both IBM and Cisco if we could have cooperated. Hubris was still rampant at IBM."

Cisco arguably pulled an "NIA" on IBM by joining with nearly all of Big Blue's competitors, including Alcatel, Hewlett-Packard, Digital, Cabletron, Cascade, and SynOptics, in the APPI Forum in 1993. Led by Cisco, the forum intended to develop an open alternative to SNA, which was owned by IBM. A year later the forum disbanded without an open system, but IBM had been weakened by the APPI Forum's efforts. By 1994, Cisco was running the SNA show, and IBM was singing a much different tune. Now it wanted a partnership with Cisco. Cisco moved its SNA development team to Research Triangle Park, North Carolina, to work directly with IBM's people. In September, Cisco and IBM announced that IBM would be giving SNA source code to Cisco, and their engineers would be working together on next-generation networking hardware.

Over the course of the following years, IBM would continue to partner with Cisco on an off-and-on basis. Basically, every time Cisco and IBM would announce an alliance, it was because IBM had been weakened to an extent that the prospect seemed tolerable.

By June 1996, Cisco had 73 percent of the IBM networking market. IBM had finally switched to IP and away from its own proprietary solutions, but it was too late. By then, Cisco had acquired Metaplex, a company in Sydney, Australia, that specialized in SNA. Paul Wood of Metaplex described IBM's last-ditch attempts to keep business from slipping through its fingers. According to Wood, IBM's revenue stream was shrinking, whereas the marketplace was, in fact, growing 25 to 30 percent per year. In frustration, IBM attempted to sabotage Cisco through the use of proprietary and patented technologies, but Cisco just reverse-engineered the protocols and moved forward.

In 1997 the love-hate relationship between IBM and Cisco raged on, but, of course, this situation couldn't continue forever. The death knell tolled on August 31, 1999, with IBM admitting the demise of its networking division. The joint Cisco-IBM press release called it an alliance, but it was an alliance that gave IBM's networking hardware division to Cisco and made IBM's customer service division support Cisco products, in return for Cisco's pledge to use IBM equipment.

➤ Switches

The next market Cisco penetrated was switches. It was clear that a large part of winning the battle for market share involved establishing beachheads for the standards Cisco promoted. Therefore, it behooved Cisco to give away its IOS when it was attempting to promulgate its standards. Later, after its protocols were accepted because of their popularity, it could use its superior knowledge of its own code to dominate the sector. Cisco wanted to begin to sell equipment to phone companies, a market dominated by switch makers in 1994. A couple of years before the StrataCom purchase, Cisco had licensed software to Cascade and 20 other companies to handle routing on telephone switches. Cisco had also tied itself more strongly to Cascade by purchasing an equity stake in the company.

Cisco formed alliances with industry leaders to complement its efforts to gain switching technology through acquisitions. In March 1993, Cisco partnered with MCI to jointly market Cisco products with MCI's HyperStream WAN switching line. It later began working with NEC, which had become a Cisco reseller in 1992, to develop ATM switches. In 1994, Cisco also allied with Northern Telecom to gain access to its Ethernet LAN switching technology. Cisco later went on to acquire companies specializing in each of the aforementioned technologies. Chambers's skill was in maintaining healthy relationships with Cisco's partners as it began to compete with them.

Madge Networks, which licensed its token-ring switching technology (a LAN technology that functioned as an alternative to Ethernet) to Cisco in March 1995, acquired Lannet Data Communications, an Ethernet switch maker and direct competitor to Cisco. Cisco had previously agreed to resell Madge's token-ring switch, but soon began missing sales targets. After Madge acquired Teleos, another competitor to Cisco products, Cisco spun around and formed a new partnership with token-ring vendor Olicom in March 1996. In August 1996, Cisco acquired Nashoba Networks to supply its own token-ring switches. Madge's stock was crushed, and Madge faced a class-action suit for "negligent, reckless, and/or intentional behavior." (On August 31, 1999, Madge Networks acquired Olicom's token-ring business.)

➤ Wintel

By 1996, the personal computer industry had exploded, as had the networking industry at large. Networking showed up on Microsoft's radar in 1996, and at the time Intel arguably owned the low-end networking market. Windows and Intel wanted to expand into the networking and corporate sphere where Cisco prevailed. Cisco knew it would be encountering Microsoft and Intel sooner or later, so alliances with both seemed to be a good idea.

Chambers was well aware of the dangers of partnerships with the two giants. He already knew that Microsoft's partnering record had been atrocious. A company allying itself with Microsoft usually ended up screwed, be it IBM, Apple, or 3Com. Then again, computer companies usually handled acquisitions poorly, and Chambers had figured out how to avoid that. Chambers, by this point in his alliance expertise, had a deep understanding of the importance and difficulties of billion-dollar strategic alliances.

In pondering the industry alliances that had worked over the years, Chambers determined that the successful ones, like that between Intel and Microsoft, worked because the companies had grown up together. Still, the two companies hated each other. Their alliance was necessary, but not happy. Another insight Chambers had was that the problems in many alliances are caused because the executives tend to be short-sighted as they divvy up the benefits, insisting that each transaction be half and half. No single transaction he's had, he says, has been 50-50. Sometimes Cisco's partner will get 70 percent of the benefit, and the next time Cisco might get 80 percent of the benefit. All in all, it adds up to 50-50. A certain amount of trust is a prerequisite as well: Often, everything moves so fast in a partnership that actions are undertaken before formal contracts are drawn.

Nevertheless, Chambers was dedicated to being as paranoid as Andy Grove, Intel's famously successful CEO. He would not be surprised if Intel or Microsoft competed with him outside the terms of any alliances he made; he only expected cooperation inside the terms of the contract.

In 1997, Cisco pushed its way into the arms of the Big Two. Microsoft's high-end operating system, Windows NT, included networking capabilities. Computer networks were managed by computers called servers, and many servers were controlled by software from Novell, the industry leader. Microsoft designed Windows NT to control those network servers (among other things) and to compete with Novell. All the servers were based on Intel microprocessors.

At the beginning of the year, Cisco's management intimated that it was on the same footing as Intel and Microsoft. "You'll have three best-in-class companies, and in the same way people have chosen Windows NT and the Pentium Pro, people also will choose Cisco IOS," boldly averred Don Listwin, senior vice president in charge of the IOS, to *Red Herring*.[2] Cisco and Microsoft soon launched a series of alliances on several fronts. First, they announced an alliance on enterprise security solutions. Large businesses needed the ability to maintain secure networks regardless of the location of the components. Enterprise networks would often use the Internet, instead of trying to build a private network across the country or overseas. But they wanted to maintain the security that a private network gives. Cisco and Microsoft collaborated to compete with the companies that dominated this sector, including Novell. Their next big push was in directory services. Directory services provide a framework for networked data that allows the system to intelligently categorize data by context. Unfortunately, directory services are very difficult to implement effectively. Cisco agreed to base its efforts on Microsoft's Active Directory software, and by September 1997 Cisco and Microsoft released a draft set of standards for integrating network management with user profiles.

Cisco, Intel, and Microsoft came together in what they called the Networked Multimedia Connection (NMC) in March 1997. Each of the companies wanted to encourage and control high-end applications for networked computers. Videoconferencing fit the bill exactly; transmitting real-time video simultaneously to many people requires expensive and complicated networks, software, and computers. Unsurprisingly, these companies wanted to be the ones selling the equipment and software to make that happen. Each company provided one piece of the puzzle: Cisco's networking hardware, Intel's chips, and Microsoft's computer software. The NMC alliance opened the first

Networked Multimedia Lab at Cisco's headquarters in April. This facility, ostensibly for the evaluation and development of multimedia networking, acted as a promotional showcase for the three companies.

Cisco did not intend to be manhandled by Microsoft and Intel, desiring all sides to be rewarded equally over time. By late 1997, there were signs of a possible conflict. Each company was working on networking software: Cisco's IOS, Intel's ProShare, and Microsoft's NetShow all overlapped, and Intel and Cisco were both hardware manufacturers whose product lines had the potential to compete.

Little more than a year passed before Intel dropped out of the alliance as it expanded its own networking hardware into competition with Cisco. Intel had always been one of the top suppliers of network cards that plugged into personal computers and allowed them to connect directly to computer networks, and it had used its monopoly in personal computer microprocessors to cripple 3Com's profits. Intel began moving up into switching, as Cisco moved down from high-end routers into the same market. The alliance between the two hardware giants was short lived. As for the software behemoth, Chambers said, "The only company that moves with our speed and directness is Microsoft, and they don't partner as well. They tend to want to dominate."[3]

■ SWITCHING FAST

Big hardware competitors like Intel and the NIA weren't Cisco's only competitors. So was the passing of time. Although the design model for routers hadn't changed much from Cisco's early days when it built them from standard equipment, the software that ran on the routers had grown over the years. Upgrades to the IOS enabled routers to handle a myriad of networking duties, including routing, multicasting, security, and load bearing. Still, the technology was changing rapidly, and switches (which don't examine the data, but whisk it along at a faster rate) were usurping the position of Cisco's original business, routers. By using specially designed application-specific integrated circuit (ASIC) hardware to process incoming frames, switches were able to switch frames much faster than routers could route packets. But they were also dumber. Routers examine data before figuring out the best way to get it to its destination; switches don't.

Nevertheless, the agility and low price of the switch attracted customers. Cisco had already made respectable headway in the switching market by acquiring switch manufacturers Crescendo, Kalpana, LightStream, Grand Junction, StrataCom, Nashoba, and Granite Systems. All in all, in fact, Cisco had been effectively leading the market with a 26 percent share. Then new switching technologies emerged in mid-1997: Layer 3 switching and Gigabit Ethernet. A Layer 3 switch was essentially a router that used technology developed for switches. Gigabit Ethernet was 1,000 times faster than regular Ethernet.

Cisco wasn't the first to come out with Layer 3 switching or Gigabit Ethernet, so a gang of pundits jumped on this opportunity to criticize Cisco for napping on the job. A naysayer at *Business Week* reported, "Cisco, the seemingly unstoppable growth engine, has begun to sputter. Its routers are running out of gas, and it's late to market with crucial new products that would help Cisco keep up with the pack."[4] But Chambers wasn't visibly unnerved. Cisco *was* working on Layer 3 switching and Gigabit Ethernet— it just wasn't at the head of the pack. Customers, he claimed, were willing to wait for Cisco to come out with the switches as part of the IOS rather than go to a competitor. This was the FUD tactic—fear, uncertainty, and doubt—an old IBM ploy. If you don't yet have the products, try to keep people from buying competing products by saying that you are going to have them soon, and yours will be better. Needless to say, this was counter to Cisco's friendly image. But Cisco's constituents voiced their support. A manager of network planning and design at Blue Cross/Blue Shield publicly declared, "We think it would make more sense to wait for the appropriate and corresponding Cisco Layer 3 switch solutions, and they're not that far off." A technology research advisor at First Union National Bank agreed: "My preference would be to wait and see what Cisco does in Layer 3 switching since we have so many Cisco routers installed."[5]

In Cisco's favor, there was some lag time before most networks were ready to replace their routers during which new products were being developed. And when Cisco's Layer 3 switching and Gigabit Ethernet did debut, they weren't sold as replacements for routers, but, rather, as additional capabilities in an expanded IOS. Corporations could implement hybrid networking solutions comprised of switches at the core surrounded by routers that directed traffic. This way, customers could either keep the smarter, slower, more costly routers they already owned or purchase new ones (to the continued advantage of Cisco's gross margins) *and* benefit from the faster, cheaper switches. Of course, to ensure that everything all worked together properly, the customer's best bet was to religiously stick to Cisco's IOS. Cisco also announced its plans for the Gigabit Switch Router, a hybrid part that, like the Layer 3 switch, would effectively combine the intelligence of a router with the speed of a switch.

■ AN IMPLICIT VICTORY

By the end of 1997, for the first time ever, Cisco derived more revenue from nonrouter products than from its routers. Earnings skyrocketed, and a 3-for-2 stock split was announced in December. Cisco had succeeded in becoming the one-stop provider of end-to-end network solutions.

The NIA didn't quite succeed as planned. By the end of 1997, only a year and a half old, it was already floundering. Some analysts speculated that it never really was anything but marketing tool against Cisco—a defensive barrier erected to prevent Cisco from ramming its proprietary technology through the standards committees. Kevin Tolly of the Tolly Group, which once had been the independent equipment tester for the NIA, chastised the NIA, observing that there seemed to be a lack of solidarity within the alliance; issues came up among the members about adhering to the charter. Enthusiasm about the project from vendors and analysts waned. As Tolly reported, the "dirty little secret of the router era of the early 1990s was that interoperability was a joke. While openness and interoperability were standard parts of every vendor's pitch, little was actually done about it. Few if any high-functionality, multivendor router networks were ever built." Tolly went on to implicitly excoriate the NIA founders by saying that those companies with a larger market share had "little to gain by helping smaller vendors prove their 'Brand X' products would work just as well—and cost much less—than, say the Cisco or Wellfleet router alternative." Furthermore, he chided, those "prominent vendors" came out with products with technologically advanced features that required networks like Cisco's. Tolly lamented, "The monopoly Cisco now holds over networking is due in no small part to the fact that it was able to convince customers that mixing equipment from different vendors would not be in their best interest—or in Cisco's."[6] Industry coalitions like the NIA rarely succeed in establishing standards. This is especially true when they are formed to keep a company with a de facto standard, whether Cisco or Microsoft, from winning. The company that simply moves the fastest, creates a solution that works, gets it to the market first, and continues to stay on top of the competition wins.

Chapter

The Virtual Corporation (1997–Present)

- THE CISCO CONNECTION ONLINE
- THE CISCO EMPLOYEE CONNECTION
- CYBERNETIC FINANCE ■ VIRTUAL MANUFACTURING
- KEEPING IT UP AND RUNNING

Most of Cisco's internal business is in the ether—that is, every process is automated online. By necessity, the corporation relies on the Internet to do everything—connect its far-flung outposts, integrate acquisitions quickly, churn out products on time, coordinate plans within and without the corporation, and instill a sense of community.

Cisco, in fact, is so physically immense that only savvy information technology can keep it limber. Beyond the headquarters in San Jose are two other main hubs—one in Research Triangle Park, North Carolina, and the other, the New England Research Center (opened in 1998), in Chelmsford, Massachusetts. Cisco also has sales offices and outposts in Australia, Africa, Asia, Canada, South America, and the Middle East. Although most acquisitions over the years have been Silicon Valley neighbors, this rule doesn't hold for all Cisco's nodes—especially those acquired in later years in northern Massachusetts, New Jersey, New Hampshire, Virginia, Texas, and Israel. Another prospective base is in Coyote Valley, Colorado, where Cisco is rumored to be planning a $1 billion expansion on a location for 20,000 more employees over the next 10 years. The increasing number of non-California acquisitions in recent years indicates an escalating confidence in Cisco's virtual business.

In order to prevent the system from ever becoming arthritic, Cisco is ironically rigid about its technology requirements. Every employee is issued a Hewlett-Packard desktop computer or a Toshiba laptop, never more than two years old. Everyone runs Windows, and every enterprise application runs on a Unix server. Every Cisco site uses the same type of voice service. All the networks use the same wiring scheme. A single department within a location operates the entire network, the desktops and the servers.

Peter Solvik, chief information officer, has been the mastermind behind Cisco's information technology since he was hired in 1992. Solvik's permanent ambition is to build and maintain an information systems department network that will reach the level of information accessibility that is required by a rapidly growing high-tech company.

Peter Solvik's department included about 1,000 people in 1998, with a budget of $300 million. He runs a department that is centrally managed, but locally funded. His budget includes network costs, software, and support, but not the business units' expenditures for information technology (IT). Cisco's systems have been completely standardized under Solvik's direction, which has eliminated the need for redundant IT support and facilitated upgrades.

■ THE CISCO CONNECTION ONLINE

Pete Solvik's best known accomplishment, both in and out of Cisco, is his development of the Cisco Connection Online (CCO). The CCO is the strongest link between Cisco and its customers. Since the days of Sandy Lerner and Len Bosack, Cisco had been selling its equipment over the ARPAnet, and later the Internet. Douglas Allred and Mark Tonneson had an official Cisco Web site up and running in 1993. This first site allowed for simple online transactions, customer support, and dialogue (as described in Chapter 2). In 1996, Peter Solvik stepped in and revolutionized it once more. He employed developers, artists, technical writers, and financial experts to revamp the entire site. It was his task to manage all the people, content, and resources that were creatively clashing and converging. Every department that works with customers—marketing, public relations, documentation, engineering, customer service, and technical support—was and remains individually responsible for building and maintaining its respective pages on the CCO. Running on Sun hardware and a Solaris operating system, the revamped Web site grossed $75 million in sales in the first 5 months it was online. By 1997, thousands had bookmarked it on their browsers.

As a legacy from its early days, the CCO is a conduit of information. The day a product debuts, all its documentation, from manuals to marketing information to press releases, is immediately posted on the CCO. Customers can report problems and submit queries. The Bug Alert feature posts information about software problems within 24 hours after they're found. Customers can search the bug navigator to find information on specific problems. Those with small businesses looking to purchase equipment and have it installed can search online databases of authorized Cisco equipment resellers.

The Cisco Marketplace site on the CCO—essentially, a dynamic online catalog—particularly prompted enthusiastic raves from customers. Its strength is that it can be employed not only to purchase equipment, but to compare and *configure* it online. Before customers were able to piece together compatible parts online, Cisco's product offerings resembled a jumble of jigsaw-puzzle pieces. Too many options made for too much confusion. The snap process of online configuration made Cisco's one-stop shopping campaign even easier for its customers—especially for resellers and those who install their own systems without the help of Cisco technicians.

In the past, one-third of all faxed orders contained errors that delayed processing. With the CCO, customers find it difficult to make purchasing mistakes. After customers plug in their Cisco configuration and account information, the system will alert them if, for example, they have selected software that isn't compatible with their hardware. Corporate customers raved when they realized that employees who would otherwise spend days completing orders for a networking project could order the whole affair online in a fraction of the time and thus have more time to actually install the network.

Customers obtain up-to-the minute pricing and speedy delivery after signing an electronic commerce record, the online equivalent of a traditional order on paper. The CCO automatically routes the request to a particular sales representative who handles the order and collects the commission.

Moreover, the CCO eliminates a lot of sundry expenses. In the past, Cisco would send software purchases to its customers on CDs, delivered overnight via FedEx. With the Software Library site on the CCO, software became simply downloadable. Over 90 percent of Cisco's software upgrades have been delivered via Internet—over 20,000 per week. Cisco saved over $500,000 per year in FedEx charges alone. Prior to the launch of Solvik's new Web site, customers had to follow up on their hardware deliveries by calling Cisco's customer service department. With the new Status Agent feature, customers can check the status of an order and receive a FedEx tracking number.

By 1998, the CCO began to bring in $1.5 billion per quarter—65 percent of the company's total revenue. In 1999, the CCO exceeded the $10 billion run rate, achieving the status of one of the top revenue-producing Web sites in the world. Such commerce provided an early boost to Internet commerce in general. The Web site also saved Cisco millions—more precisely, over $250 million annually—in IT services. Another way to look at the money saved, Peter Solvik pointed out, is that Cisco was thus able to spend $250 million more a year on research and development than its competitors.

The CCO has won recognition in *CIO Magazine*'s Web Business 50/50 Awards in both the Internet and Intranet categories in 1997, 1998, and 1999. In 1998, the Web Marketing Association WebAwards called the CCO "the backbone of the World Wide Web today, setting the standard for all corporate Web sites to follow."

■ THE CISCO EMPLOYEE CONNECTION

Cisco was one the first companies to create an extensive corporate intranet—a private network contained within the business, consisting of many interlinked local-area networks. The main purpose of an intranet is to share company information and computing resources among employees. Cisco's intranet—the Cisco Employee Connection (CEC)—is Peter Solvik's second-best-known contribution to the company. Ever since its conception in 1994, the CEC has been evolving, offering more and more worldwide services, until it now supports over 1.7 million pages.

Akin to the CCO, the CEC site brings disparate groups into a community and provides internal services that connect Cisco's farthest Asian outpost with the San Jose headquarters. Unlike the intranets at other companies, where the information comes from one dedicated source, the CEC is dynamic and collaborative. Executives and managers announce new acquisitions and make staff announcements. Chefs post daily menus. One-quarter of the content comes from directly from employees who post news or hold discussions online.

The CEC is far less expensive to develop, deploy, and update than traditional client/server applications. Furthermore, it works universally on all three major platforms—Windows, Macintosh, and Unix—without expensive equipment and servicing. Because it's Internet-based, the CEC doesn't need to be installed and is constantly current. The benefits of the CEC are obvious and bounteous. Not only does the CEC cultivate a sense of community and boost morale, it also whittles down the bureaucracy normally associated with a company of Cisco's breadth and depth. To boot, it cuts paper, mailing, and telephone costs—a phenomenon that immediately affects the bottom line.

Dozens of departments within Cisco contribute to the CEC, each with managers and staff who have the opportunity to contribute items of interest on demand. In order to ensure a consistent look, feel, and navigational structure, each department and business unit designates its own intranet content to application developers who work within Cisco's three-tiered intranet development infrastructure.

Several specific benefits of the system to the virtual corporation are instant communications, human resources, and general resources.

➤ Instant Communications

The CEC, and the CCO Web site at large, foster instant global communications. As soon as new product and pricing lists debut, they are available worldwide. Cisco's sales force, direct customers, and sales partners can access all information about the status of customers' orders. The site contains all the necessary data on shipment dates, backlog status reports, line-item details about each product on order, addresses, and order shipment status. This feature of the Web site makes the sales force privy to timely information and proactive in tracking orders, and reassures customers regarding orders and schedules.

Each department has its own site featuring business unit announcements. Rather than saving documents on their own computers, Ciscoans save their files to their group's Web site. If they need to present something at a meeting, they simply print out the Web site. Group interaction, therefore, is supported by the Web site.

In order to emphasize a sense of community, each of the three key areas of the company—sales, engineering, and management—can refer to a specific site within the CEC for serious dialogue and chatting. Employees worldwide communicate in proprietary newsgroups and "break rooms," where employees discuss company plans, spread gossip, and perform technological showdowns.

➤ Human Resources

The first thing that new Cisco employees are introduced to is the CEC. The moment they sit down at their new desks and turn on their new computers, the CEC screen pops up. With the number of new recruits and acquisition personnel averaging 1,000 per quarter, the CEC is a vital tool for integration. IT staff, managers, and coworkers alike are notified about new personnel through the CEC. New hires are provided with a New Hire Dashboard site, a console that provides them with everything from payroll to benefits information. Each dashboard is customized for the new employee's particular role. Sales employees receive 10-day starter kits that include in-house contact information, product data, and sales training. New Cisco marketers receive customized sets of contacts and connections.

Human resources information is ubiquitous for all employees. News bits, forms, and files regarding company events, health registration, and expense-tracking reports can be accessed and downloaded on demand. If employees choose to enroll in a training class, they can register anytime, anywhere online and the CEC will automatically route the approval forms to their managers, enroll them in the class, and send them an e-mail that confirms their enrollment. The CEC is so customized that when an employee informs the system that she is pregnant, she is provided with such information as new payroll benefit and deduction forms.

➤ General Resources

The CEC offers delights from the utilitarian to the exotic. Due to Cisco's partnerships with broadcast organizations, Cisco employees can check traffic and weather conditions before the commute home. Reports of company events are highlighted, as well as industry trends and news flashes. World news and regional reports are displayed, as well as details particular to a staff member's specific location. If an employee is assigned to work or attend a meeting in another Cisco location, the CEC will provide a floor plan, a cafeteria menu and, if available, directions to the onsite gym. Employees with Cisco stock options can check on their stock status.

Those going on business trips can log into the Java-powered Metro application, which automates travel arrangements and enables travelers to track their expense accounts. The SABRE travel system, integrated seamlessly into CEC's Metro, enables employees to book their own (frugal coach-class) reservations, as well as car rentals and hotel reservations. If an employee uses an American Express corporate card for a trip, or any other applicable purchase, Metro can access and display all the credit charges. The employee selects all those relevant to the expense report, and the employee's checking account is automatically reimbursed within 48 hours.

For employees who are having difficulty with their office equipment or with a product, the CEC hosts a site dedicated to IT. Staff members can report problems with the phones, computer hardware, or software at the Cisco Technical Response Center, then review the status of their requests or alter them if the problems change. The CEC routes all requests to the proper support centers at the respective location.

The CEC even provides an option for Ciscophilic employees: Staff members who want to advertise the company on their downtime can order company coffee mugs and T-shirts via the corporate gear site.

■ CYBERNETIC FINANCE

Larry Carter, Cisco's chief financial officer, had one main goal when he joined in 1995: to shorten the end-of-quarter close and cut spending on finance. He believed that shortening the 10-day closing period would improve the reliability and efficiency of his department. Carter intended that his staff would take less time to produce better numbers. This would only be possible if the data they needed was immediately available.

Larry Carter told Peter Solvik, the chief information officer, that he had too many people focused ineffectively. He didn't have good information and, he griped, the organization was not effectively supporting the company. Carter then invested nearly all increases in his departmental budget into IT.

The information systems (IS) department responded by developing an online system that would allow Cisco's accountants to see the company's transactions with as little lag time as possible. The Executive Information System (EIS), integrated into Cisco's intranet, provided managers and executives with booking, billings, and backlog information for all of Cisco's transactions. Similarly, the Web-based Decision Support System (DSS) delivered customizable sales-tracking reports to authorized personnel. The process was difficult, but by 1998 Carter's initiatives had taken effect. His budget, which in 1995 had been 2 percent of sales, was only 1 percent of sales in

1998. With the online financial information, the closing period took only two days.

Larry Carter realized that there were unintended advantages to being online. He could get, among other data, information on revenues, margins, orders, discounts on the orders, and the top customers from the previous day. The orders were directly connected to information about the salespeople who handled the transactions. Carter and Chambers could oversee sales and send feedback directly to the salespeople. Carter reveled in the direct communication. He and Chambers would fire out nice and not-so-nice missives to various department heads. This was the kind of powerful application of networking that Cisco loved to trumpet in its incessant campaign to show that it represents the golden ideal of the modern business. It truly did reap visible rewards, allowing Cisco to adjust sales targets or hire new employees when the daily information revealed market change, months before its competitors were able to react.

■ VIRTUAL MANUFACTURING

What Cisco does best is running a corporation of networked engineers, marketers, programmers, salespeople, and technicians who build and sell equipment. Back at the crucial juncture in 1992, Morgridge, Chambers and the executive team determined that suppliers added more value than Cisco in the area of manufacturing. Cisco itself would focus on its core abilities—corporate strategy, engineering, design, marketing, and customer service—and hire other companies to build the equipment. Carl Redfield, then senior vice president of manufacturing, determined that Cisco didn't add value by having multiple people touch the product.

One of the best reasons to outsource manufacturing is that Cisco can remain more flexible in its choice of technology because it has not invested a lot of capital in one type of facility. Many of the finished products never even cross a Cisco building's threshold. In fact, Cisco hires other manufacturing companies to produce about 70 to 80 percent of everything it sells. Through the 1990s, Cisco established partnerships with several contract equipment manufacturing companies (CEM) such as Jabil Circuit Inc. of Saint Petersburg, Florida, and distributors such as Avnet Inc. of Great Neck, New York.

Cisco would not be able to outsource as efficiently and successfully without its pioneering use of the intranet and extranet. Not only was Cisco one of the first companies to create an intranet, it was one of the first to extend it into an *extranet,* a means of communicating with customers, suppliers, and partners. Chief Information Officer Peter Solvik and his team have automated the entire manufacturing and shipment process. In fact, the technology has enabled subcontractors like Jabil and Avnet to become part of a single enterprise with Cisco. By using networked applications to integrate suppliers, Cisco in effect created a *single enterprise.* Manufacturers act like adjunct Cisco manufacturing sites as they respond to customer orders without the time-consuming hierarchical system of receiving orders from the mother company. Cisco saves millions in processing, inventory, and delivery costs by having the manufacturers receive and deliver orders. By outsourcing most of its manufacturing, Cisco actually pays 30 percent less than it would cost to assemble the products itself.

The manufacturing process actually begins when customers access the Cisco Connection Online and configure their systems. The product configuration is routed to Cisco's order entry and scheduling database. Cisco's scheduling system looks at product-available and product-promised data, checking for the first available time slot for the order. The Oracle-powered order management system then translates that data into a parts order for companies like Jabil and Avnet. Because the online configurator decreases mishaps, the order is now usually correct; in fact, only about 2 percent of orders need any reworking before the job can be initiated.

Half of the customer orders from the Web go *directly* to Cisco's contractors (over $10 million in business per day) with the built-to-order (BTO) specifications determined by the customer. They simply look up the specs for routers, switches, and other networking gear on a specialized CCO site called the Manufacturing Connection Online (MCO), part of the Single Enterprise Program that sets up subcontractors as an extension of the Cisco factory.

CEMs usually follow the blueprints drafted by Cisco engineers, although there are some exceptions to this rule. In Taiwan, the subcontractors sometimes partner with Cisco engineers to create original product designs. Local partnerships of engineers and manufacturers also abound. When Cisco China won the contract to supply wide-area network switches to China's National Financial Network, it teamed up with Zhongyan, a local systems integrator that supplied and installed the switches. Cisco Canada has likewise established its own local manufacturing partnerships with circuit board manufacturers. The network enables Cisco and its partners to respond to each other and to customers' demands in real time.

Cisco has borrowed a strategy from Japan. It has effectively created a Japanese-style *keiretsu,* in which several companies work together to provide products for customers. This is all coordinated through the extranet.

As part of the Cisco Enterprise Program—the manufacturing resource planning (MRP) system on the extranet—subcontractors will often purchase materials from other suppliers to build full assemblies. For example, CEM Jabil will buy parts from distributor Avnet and combine them with parts from its own stockrooms as needed to make Cisco boards. Avnet and Jabil work together directly due to the relationship that Cisco has created between them. Once assembly is completed at either plant, the system automatically prompts Cisco to pay for the parts and construction.

Cisco engineers likewise benefit from the technology implemented in this manufacturing program. Usually, four or five iterations of a prototype design are required—with each prototype taking an average of one week to complete. A great deal of the week would be spent gathering and disseminating the information to other engineers working on the same product line. Cisco developed the new product information (NPI) database in order to reduce the time spent gathering product information from one day to approximately 15 minutes, with a similar ratio for the time spent distributing it. Altogether, the NRI database saves up to half of an engineer's time. This time savings alone—translating into an estimated $100 million annually—boosts the time allocated to research and development. And the technology solidifies the connection between the onsite engineer and the adjunct manufacturer.

Cisco suppliers also use the CCO's enterprise resource planning (ERP) system to run their own production lines. On a weekly basis, the subcontractors receive an updated 12-month forecast that gives them a window on how to allocate their own production capacity. Several of Cisco's CEMs build subassemblies directly from Cisco's demand forecasts and supply that equipment to all product lines. Annual savings on this account alone are more than $35 million, due to labor avoidance and reduction in material cost. With direct links to its manufacturers, Cisco can streamline procurement, eliminate paper orders, save time, and expedite delivery. Purchasing staff can then focus on more strategic activities, such as negotiating, partnership, and business development.

➤ Direct Delivery

Before online supply automation, Cisco manufacturers would stockpile excess inventory in order to compensate for expected delays and errors in order requests. Because real-time information on sales requests and inventory levels is constantly online and available to Cisco and its manufacturers, Cisco can maintain lower inventory levels without increasing the risk of part shortages. Direct delivery from the factory cuts lead times at least in half—from four or five weeks to two. As a result of the inventory on-line connection, Cisco has reduced its own inventory by 45 percent, saving $5.6 million. No paperwork is involved in the process until Cisco receives its check in the mail—which, in itself, will soon become an anachronism as Pete Solvik's team sets up an e-payment system.

➤ European Supply Chain Success

Up until 1997, Cisco San Jose and Cisco Europe were experiencing great difficulty in managing their distribution systems. A hundred different carriers were coming to Cisco's doors to pick up all the equipment and parts that weren't manufactured in Europe. To make matters worse, sales of networking equipment began to skyrocket around the same time. Each carrier had its own paperwork and preferences, making shipping a cumbersome and expensive proposition. In April 1997, Cisco decided to winnow the number of carriers down to three—to be managed by one, UPS Worldwide Logistics (UPS-WL). Cisco signed a $2 million contract for UPS-WL to manage the entire European arm of its product supply chain. Part of the deal meant getting the equipment out of Cisco's California warehouses and into Europe as quickly as possible. Cisco would ship hardware to UPS-WL's distribution center in Best, the Netherlands, where the carrier would cross-dock the products and ship them out via the other carriers.

UPS-WL then became a clearinghouse of sorts, with a steady stream of deliveries from San Jose. With deliveries on a consistent schedule, Cisco's European customers now receive their orders in four days from the point of manufacture. As a result, Cisco has been able to cut costs, improve operating efficiencies, and track inventory better.

■ KEEPING IT UP AND RUNNING

At Cisco, technical support is also called *customer advocacy*. The primary function of customer advocacy has always been to keep the technology up and running. It was a powerful idea to name the technical support department Customer Advocacy. Usually, technical support is regarded like a team of plumbers and electricians, to be called in when customers make mistakes, break things, or can't figure things out. As customer advocacy, technical support is more like a team of butlers that serves the customers' needs and broadcasts their opinions.

Technical support was much simpler when Cisco sold only a few products. As it diversified and began to sell many different types of equipment, the equation became much more complicated. It was necessary to avoid thrusting customers into the tedious bureaucracy that often appeared in the technical support departments of large companies. Rather than create specialized technical support departments for each product, Chambers instead strengthened the capabilities of Cisco's centralized technical support system.

Cisco maintained responsive technical support in three ways. First, Cisco worked hard to make products that were highly reliable and easy to use. Especially in high-end routers, where the company has enjoyed huge profit margins and overwhelming market share, Cisco was able to afford to put money into making highly reliable equipment. This high reliability endeared them to resellers, especially those who give their beeper numbers to customers and don't care for calls at 4 A.M. As Cisco began to move into the telecommunications industry, it found the bar to be raised much higher. Phone equipment requires a much higher standard of reliability. Cisco has struggled both to provide this reliability and to convince carriers that it could provide it. The technical support staff at Cisco, no doubt, still earn their money.

Second, Cisco developed well-trained technical staff across the globe. The Cisco Networking Academy and Cisco University programs trained people to use Cisco gear; the students became resellers, network managers, and Cisco employees, including technical support staff. Cisco opened central support offices called technical assistance centers around the globe, at its headquarters in San Jose, and throughout Europe, the Pacific Rim, and Latin America. Because they were centrally managed by the vice presidents of global support engineering and worldwide service technical support under the senior vice president of customer advocacy, the technical assistance centers were able to serve all customers equally well. As with the British Empire, the sun never sets on Cisco technical support. A call from New York at 1 A.M. could be routed to Sydney, where normal work hours would be under way. The technical assistance centers were complemented by smaller, localized offices. As early as 1995, for example, Cisco opened a local support office in the Philippines. Later Asian investments included $6 million for a fourth technical assistance center in Beijing, in 1999.

Third, Cisco incorporated comprehensive technical support into the Cisco Connection Online, reducing the need for support staff and reducing the demand on engineers' time. By 1997, Cisco asserted that its Web site was handling 70 percent of technical support needs. In 1999, Cisco overtook 3Com in a reseller satisfaction survey conducted by *Computer Reseller News,* particularly because of advances in product reliability and in its technical support. One reseller was quoted as saying that he never really had to call Cisco's technical support because he got everything off of the Web site.[1]

Chapter

The New Battle (1996–1998)

In 1996, Chambers started discussing his belief that the Internet could be used to carry telephone calls. He realized that the future of telephony was over IP networks, a technology called *voice over IP* (VoIP in the acronym-happy networking world). The explosion of the World Wide Web convinced him that the future of all communications was over the Internet and similar networks. So, he set out to make Cisco able to handle VoIP technology.

Cisco started using its own internal network to make international calls, reducing its long-distance phone bills significantly. After Cisco put in a direct network to send data to and from its offices in Japan, it had enough capacity left to send its phone calls over that network, as well. Chambers loved the savings when Cisco's overseas outposts called headquarters. "It saves me $30,000 a month in Japan," Chambers gloated, "because I already had the data line, and the majority of the time I've got extra capacity on it, at a dramatically lower cost." The network was expensive, but Chambers claimed that the data transfer alone justified its cost, effectively providing free VoIP. Soon thereafter, Chambers became a big proponent of free phone calls on the Internet. It was a big deal, and led to his decision to start selling Cisco's Internet technology to phone companies.

According to Chambers, digital data is New World and the circuits of voice infrastructure are Old World. These worlds converge as voice and data become one and the same. Chambers envisions that video, television, radio, and interactive entertainment will also be transmitted over this one giant global network. While companies like Lucent Technologies, Nortel, and others have been acquiring infrastructure and laying the foundation to move to data networking, Chambers likes to insist that Cisco, which has been devoted to data all along, will be the company to deliver the new infrastructure. The New World Network, he says, will converge the Internet with telecom's high-speed fiber-optic, cable, and wireless systems. The Internet will be everything: the World Wide Web, the phone lines (calls will be free), the conveyor and purveyor of music and video. Thousands of new devices and gizmos combining worldwide phone service with e-commerce capabilities, the Web, video e-mail, and more will emerge into the market, requiring some way to make them all compatible with each other. The Internet will be the conduit. And, as Chambers declares, the Internet is virtually Cisco.

■ CHANGING THE SYSTEM

In order to ensure that the company would be able to prepare for the future, Chambers decided to implement another organizational overhaul. Up until this point, Cisco had been suffering from the problems of too much decentralization: Product marketing was not synchronized, and

IOS implementation was becoming difficult because the many engineering teams were forced to compromise on the abilities of their products. Cisco had already been selling to new kinds of customers other than the traditional corporate enterprise market, which was principally corporations and big organizations. Internet service providers, small offices, and home offices were also in Cisco's market for networking equipment. Chambers wanted to add telephone companies to the register. He envisioned Cisco as not only the backbone of the Internet, but of the entire communications industry.

First, Chambers converged all the autonomous business units into three lines of business, one for each of Cisco's target markets: enterprises, small to medium businesses, and service providers. Each line of business was comprised of business units, network management units, and marketing units. Chambers selected his most effective business unit managers to head each line: Mario Mazzola for the enterprise line, Howard Charney for the small/medium business line, and Don Listwin for the service provider line. The enterprise line was considered the core, with its array of high-end equipment and wide-area network technology. The small/medium business line was a first foray into the market of cable modem and high-speed connection software for small businesses and home offices. The service provider line, however, would be Cisco's most ambitious: the crux where networking would meet telephony.

The customers for products in the service provider line included telecommunications carriers (phone companies), Internet service providers, cable companies, and wireless companies. Cisco had already made inroads into the Internet service provider market, which depended upon Cisco's routers. However, the giant telecommunications industry was a whole different ballgame. This was a brand-new business for Cisco. Once it just sold companies equipment for internal networks, then equipment for the Internet. Now it was selling to phone companies, the companies that connected people to the Internet.

Phone companies had been buying switches that were manufactured by the likes of long-time telecommunications equipment providers Lucent (an outgrowth and inheritor of AT&T's Bell Labs) and Northern Telecom, along with Cisco's datacom competitors Newbridge Networks and Ascend. Carriers, like ISPs, also cared about network management, an area in which Cisco had been weak. Most important, telecommunications carriers had completely different expectations for equipment than the companies in Cisco's traditional market. They wanted superreliable equipment that provided dependable, high-quality connections. Cisco was accustomed to staying on the bleeding edge of technology, making less reliable but more flexible equipment. Chambers believed that Cisco would be able to claw its way to the top with its superior understanding of the demands of data networking.

■ LAYING THE LINES

The groundwork for Cisco's move into telecom had actually been laid with its move into switching, especially with its acquisitions of Crescendo and StrataCom. Telecommunication has always depended on high-speed switching to open lines between parties. Before 1996, Cisco's interest in switches was mostly limited to those in the packet networks it understood, ones that let computers trade bits with each other. When Cisco began looking at telecommunications carriers, the lords of the circuit-based networks, as potential customers, Chambers knew the company needed to rapidly expand its abilities. Fortunately for Cisco, everyone wanted to move to packet-based networks, if only someone would provide equipment that worked.

Even though most analysts saw fellow datacom players such as 3Com, Cabletron, Ascend, and Bay Networks as Cisco's primary competitors, Chambers knew that the inevitable convergence of data and voice networks would cause the two industries to coalesce. Cisco topped all its data competitors and was a better-run company. Competing telecom managers could handle multibillion-dollar companies for the long haul, but didn't have datacom know-how. What Chambers had to worry about was time; he had to act before his datacom competitors became subsidiaries of the telecom players.

Cisco was ready to tackle the big boys. It had to be able to advance on several fronts at the same time, as it expanded into new markets. Cisco had mastered the process of moving into a new space at the top of market share back in the early 1990s. It identified all the major players, but especially concentrated on innovative start-ups and watched what they were doing. Chambers devised a multiphase development strategy. At each phase, Cisco would introduce new products and services. If internal research and development was unable to meet the timeline, Cisco would acquire new companies.

Starting in 1997, soon after the business reorganization, Cisco invoked long-term strategies to move into all areas of telecommunications, from the end user to the network backbone. Cisco made its move into the hot consumer and small-business market for digital subscriber line (DSL) equipment. DSL is a technology that allows high-speed data connections over existing phone lines. For big business, the brass ring was *multiservice,* products that could handle both large loads of data and phone service. Optical internetworking was the lifeblood of the telecom networks. Telecommunications carriers, from AT&T to Qwest, owned vast networks of optical fiber. Companies like Lucent had the technology to handle fiber-optic switching, but Cisco's equipment simply couldn't connect to fiber. To gobble up market share, Cisco gobbled up companies.

➤ Digital Subscriber Line (DSL)

Cisco's move into DSL was fairly painless and economical. With four small acquisitions in the space of a year and a half, Cisco went from having no DSL solution to becoming the provider of that equipment to major carriers like US West. Cisco acquired the privately held company Telesend on March 3, 1997, and was able to release a product from the acquisition on March 26. In July, Cisco's acquisition of Dagaz, a subsidiary of Integrated Network Corporation under Dev Gupta, extended its capabilities into international markets. Solomon D. Trujillo, CEO of US West, recommended to Chambers that Cisco acquire NetSpeed International. Trujillo liked the company's products, but didn't want to buy from a start-up. Chambers, listening to his customers (as he has since day one at Cisco), bought the company for $326 million in March 1998. On August 18, 1999, Cisco acquired MaxComm of Chelmsford, Massachusetts, and its consumer DSL technology for $143 million. MaxComm was a Cisco Kid from the start: It was founded by Gupta in 1998.

High-speed connections to the home and small office currently come through three avenues: phone lines, wireless, and cable. Cisco complemented its DSL spree with two acquisitions. It snapped up Clarity Wireless of Belmont, California, on September 15, 1998, for $157 million. Cisco has not moved strongly into the wireless market, relying on alliances with industry heavyweights. Cisco's cable products and solutions group went farther afield with its acquisition, exactly a year later, of 66-employee Cocom A/S of Denmark—a steal at $65.6 million. Cocom supplied Cisco's cable group with international flavor and ability.

➤ Multi-service

Most of Cisco's recent acquisitions have been in pursuit of its multi-service initiative, to provide voice and data products. Cisco desperately wanted to be able to provide voice and video service over its data networks. Cisco began selling the concept as a way of avoiding long-distance charges: It's the Internet, it's free! But the reality goes deeper. Lucent, Nortel, and many smaller companies were moving into this nascent market from every side, and Chambers wanted Cisco to be on top.

In 1997, Cisco began its foray into the multi-service market with the acquisition of Ardent, intended to advance the abilities of the StrataCom line. Cisco had two seats on Ardent's board from the start, and micromanaged the engineers. Volpi later admitted that the acquisition didn't work out that well.[1] The Virginia company Light-Speed International met with Cisco in December, intending to discuss licensing of its packet-based call control software, but instead agreed to a $196 million acquisition within 3 hours.

In 1998, Cisco went whole hog, snapping up companies that might give it a viable VoIP package. Precept Software (with Judy Estrin and William Carrico), the Israeli company CLASS Data Systems, and the New England companies Summa Four and American Internet Corporation were acquired within a 5-month span, for a total of $307 million. These software-strong start-ups gave Cisco the ability to handle multiservice networks of about 100 people by November 1998, good enough to start selling product, but nowhere near the capacity of tens of thousands it wanted. Selsius, a Texas affiliate of the French conglomerate LargardËre, started Cisco on track toward handling legacy phone systems when it was acquired in October; the first fruits of the deal were realized in March 1999.

➤ Fiber-Optic

At the top end, Cisco needed to transform itself into a credible supplier of high-end fiber-optic equipment. A five-phase plan was designed in 1997, and Cisco went to work. Two years, $8 billion in acquisitions, and undisclosed expenditures on internal research later, Cisco was able to enter the market. Cisco started small, buying 40-employee Skystone Systems of Ottawa for $92 million in June 1997 to enable its routers and switches to hook up to fiber-optic lines. With the $126 million acquisition of Pipelinks in December 1998, Cisco stepped up to integrating the optical network protocols into its routers. Granite Systems' Gigabit Ethernet equipment, crucial to Cisco's optical strategy, was finally ready for market, 18 months later than originally expected. Although that kind of delay isn't uncommon in the industry, the Granite Systems acquisition turned out to be a pie in the face because Cisco was momentarily behind the curve.

➤ Encryption

Cisco wanted to be the first to build the complex security and prioritization software and hardware necessary to private networks. It's certainly to Cisco's advantage to push this solution, as it requires more complex and expensive equipment than traditional wide-area networks. Also, this initiative acts as a test case for technology and services that Cisco eventually intends to use throughout its product line. However, the benefits, once the technology is up to par, are actual.

To make this program a reality, Cisco has beefed up on security and formed alliances with other companies. In June 1997, Cisco acquired the Global Internet Software Group for its security software. WheelGroup Corporation, acquired in February 1998, added network monitoring to the package.

■ BOOSTING THE BRAND

Nineteen ninety-eight was a banner year for Cisco. Cisco had over 14,500 employees and had increased revenue 31 percent over the previous fiscal year. On July 19, Cisco's stock price spiked yet another $4 higher, and Cisco surged past its $100 billion milestone in market value. The hundreds of stock option millionaires at Cisco became still richer. CEO John Chambers's holdings skipped up to about $100 million. The *Wall Street Journal* article that trumpeted Cisco's achievement noted that Cisco reached this mark after just 12 years in business—believed to be the fastest acceleration of market capitalization ever. Microsoft, in contrast, took 20 years to reach the same threshold.

By 1998, 7 people were gaining Internet access every second, and 10 times as many messages were delivered via Cisco technology than through the U.S. postal service. John Chambers gleefully reported that his 74-year-old father, who hadn't known what the Internet was two years before, had since logged on and found so much investment research online that he had begun to give Chambers advice on how to run Cisco. In the 1998 annual report, Chambers emphasized the often-overlooked fact that Cisco products were likely to have played a key role in transferring just about any e-mail sent over the Internet. Eighty percent of all data sent over the Internet, in fact, was said to have been transmitted through Cisco equipment. Analysts attributed Cisco's untrammeled success to its one-stop product line, its aggressive marketing, its outstanding support services, and of course, its dynamic leader, John T. Chambers.

As Cisco achieved star status, its CEO, by necessity, came to the forefront. Back in 1996, when Chambers first became CEO, he had adopted John Morgridge's understated style in the public eye. "Neither John Morgridge nor I had a particular desire to be real visible," claimed John. "It wasn't one of the things that motivated us." Then came rapid success and rampant attention. *Fortune, Business Week,* the *Wall Street Journal, Forbes, Wired*—editors converged on San Jose to see and speak with Cisco's esteemed leader.

Chambers decided that it would be advantageous to show his face more. The small/medium business division was one reason for Chambers to focus on the smaller customers—even the average consumer. The majority of the division's products would be purchased indirectly, and Chambers wanted customers to ask for Cisco products by name. Chambers therefore followed Bill Gates's lead and went out as a Johnny Appleseed figure for the company, spreading and sowing Cisco's good word. "I really don't like it," he claimed in one interview. "I'd rather spend time with customers or internally here than doing interviews or other things." He always insisted that he did it only for the good of the company. "You can have the best products, the best service organization in the world, the best strategy, but if the products are being consumed indirectly and the people who are asking for the vendor selection don't know that, they aren't going to ask for Cisco."[2]

To some extent, all this is probably true. But have no doubt—he relishes the limelight with a passion. Everyone comments on his good cheer and genuine kindness. "I believe nice people can win," he declares matter-of-factly. He allows journalists and television crews to follow his apron-clad self around Cisco headquarters as he generously distributes ice cream to the employees and natters on about Cisco's achievements. His interest in his employees and customers is genuine, although his rallying speeches for corporate togetherness and idealistic platitudes about changing the world are sometimes difficult to believe. He's on a perennial sales call, perhaps, and, by being open, he's constantly trying to close.

Cisco's television ads are a strong reflection of Cisco's own view of a nearly utopian future, brought to you by Cisco. Building on Chambers's momentum, in 1998 Cisco's marketing department began launching ads with his memorable slogan, "Are you ready?" The idea was to make Cisco a household name as Lucent had done with its own television ads after it split from AT&T (everyone recognizes the red brush stroke O). Cisco was willing to spend $30 million for prime-time exposure.

One spot, entitled "The Mouths of Babes," featured a succession of children from a panoply of lands and cultures (Vietnam, England, Spain, etc.) spouting sentence fragments: "One day . . . the Internet will make . . . long-distance calls . . . a thing of the past . . . *Are you ready? . . . Are you ready? . . . Are you ready? . . .*" After the kids speak, the voice-over booms, "Virtually all Internet traffic travels along the systems of one company, Cisco Systems. Empowering the Internet generation."

The spots, proclaimed Corporate Marketing Vice President Keith Fox, were only part of a multitiered marketing effort. Fox's intent was also to boost Cisco's brands: Cisco-Powered Network for ISP customers and Cisco NetWorks for consumer electronics firms that buy Cisco technology for cable modems. The Cisco NetWorks campaign also included a marketing program that enabled companies using Cisco products to affix a Cisco NetWorks label on their computers, televisions, or other devices, in much the same way that enterprise customers can put a Cisco-Powered Network icon on their equipment or personal computer makers can put Intel Inside stickers on their computers. The strategy was to make Cisco a household name, brand Cisco technology just as Intel brands its microprocessors, equate the Cisco brand with the Internet itself, and associate the Internet with good things like global togetherness. "What's exciting to me about this technology is not the technology itself," Chambers declared, "It's the way it's leveling the playing fields between big companies and little companies; and big countries and little countries."[3]

Chambers has become politically conscious and wants government to "get it," as he puts it, referring to Cisco's promise of the future of the Internet. He frequently drops the names of presidents and heads of states with whom he has recently met: Bill Clinton and Al Gore, George W. Bush (to whose campaign he contributes a great deal of money), China's Jiang Zemin, and British Prime Minister Tony Blair among them. He has served on President Clinton's Committee for Trade Policy and is deeply involved with a Silicon Valley lobbying group known as TechNet. Everything is inextricably linked: the economy, competitiveness of business, employment levels, overall well-being, and reelection results. Security litigation and encryption are key issues Chambers has pegged for the next election. High tech, he asserts, is critical to the future well-being of the U.S. economy.

"You have three choices," Chambers said of a high-technology company's methods of operation. "You either move quickly and bet you're building to win, or you move slower and a little safer, but you probably never have the chance to get the market share you want. Or you do nothing. . . ."

A usually cynical press would not be so willing to highlight all of Chambers's hopes of bringing about a wonderful new world had not the company been so spectacularly successful. Chambers's success lends him credibility (or, Cisco's success lends Chambers credibility).

The editors and journalists who heard all the publicity, came to speak to the courtly cover boy Chambers, and witnessed Cisco's numbers obviously liked what they saw. By the end of 1998, *Forbes ASAP* deemed Cisco the country's most dynamic company. *Fortune* named it one of the 25 best companies to work for in the United States. *Network World* esteemed Cisco "the most powerful company" and Chambers "the most powerful CEO in the industry." *Business Week* named Chambers one of the top executives worldwide. *Upside* magazine ranked him "the top titan of the digital world." And Cisco got publicity from the top. At a White House event, President Clinton and Vice President Al Gore adulated Cisco, calling it "one of the most respected companies, not in [the networking] field, but in any field." Chambers, they asserted, is "a true leader in this industry." *Worth* named Chambers the number-two CEO in America, and *Business 2.0* ranked Cisco number one in its report on the "Top 100 Hottest Companies on the Net."

■ CORPORALS AND CAPTAINS

John Chambers says he'd really like the attention and credit to be directed at the team. So he mentions them frequently in his interviews, particularly the executive nucleus of 17 or so vice presidents that directly report to him and the people that directly report to them, some 50-odd more vice presidents. President Clinton once joked with Chambers about the number of people with executive positions working one or two layers below him. "I always liked John Chambers," Clinton remarked, "until I found out that he had 70 vice presidents. I don't know what to make of that. That he's more important than I am? He's less efficient than I am?"[4]

The top spots commonly go to presidents and CEOs from the companies that Cisco has acquired. This has created an extraordinarily rich pool of talent within Cisco's top ranks. Chambers is a conductor leading one of the industry's most talented orchestras. He has a management team made up of some of the country's most successful entrepreneurs. Stock options and Cisco's ever-escalating stock price no doubt keep many of these entrepreneurs on board. But so do Chambers's ability to delegate and his willingness to listen to the opinions of others. Cisco is truly not run by Chambers alone. He has appointed crucial functions to some of the brightest entrepreneurs in Silicon Valley.

One such executive is Judy Estrin, Cisco's chief technology officer. Judy came to Cisco via the acquisition of Precept Software, her and her husband William Carrico's multimedia desktop software company, in March 1998. Precept equipment would go into the small/medium business line, of which Carrico became vice president when Charney stepped down. As CTO, Estrin's position is higher than her husband's. Ed Kozel, her predecessor, became senior vice president of corporate development soon after her arrival at Cisco. Estrin and Carrico have long been famous figures in Silicon Valley as founders of Bridge Communications, a pioneer in networking and an early competitor to Cisco. Chambers has made Estrin one of his star executives. She is the visionary whose job is to guide the development and acquisition of the technology that will fulfill Chambers's strategic vision for Cisco. Part of Estrin's vision of Cisco's technology includes making the network infrastructure upgrades that result from streaming in applications for distance learning or desktop television. So far, the Internet Protocol (IP) seems to be Estrin's choice for transmission because it can work with many technologies—ATM, Gigabit Ethernet, token ring, and asymmetric digital subscriber line (ADSI).

Larry Carter, Cisco's chief financial officer since 1995, plays the critical role of maintaining Cisco's famously Spartan frugality. You won't find Cisco executives luxuriating in perks like country club memberships and company cars, first-class plane tickets, and single hotel rooms at off-site meetings. In an interview in *CFO Magazine,* Carter noted that the trap many companies get in is that they're too internally focused and forget who pays the bills. The chief financial officer's job is to "balance all the moving parts" of the organization—to build a quality team in finance, run a low-cost organization, accelerate the monthly close, generate financial reports, and improve productivity per finance department employee.

The collaboration between Gary Daichendt, executive vice president of worldwide operations, and Chambers goes back to their days together at IBM. Daichendt has a career history that has nearly paralleled Chambers's. Before joining Cisco, Daichendt spent 10 years at IBM in sundry sales, marketing, and management positions. Then he, like his boss, jumped ship for Wang, where he held the positions of vice president of central operations and vice president of worldwide marketing. As vice president of worldwide operations he is responsible for Cisco's sales, distribution, manufacturing, and global alliances.

He travels worldwide and presses flesh with Cisco counterparts abroad, opens new networking academies (see Chapter 5), and scouts out new places to launch Cisco nodes.

Mario Mazzola was president and CEO of Crescendo until Cisco bought his company in 1994. Like Estrin, Mazzola has an entrepreneurial streak: He cofounded Crescendo and, before that, was a cofounder and VP of David Systems. Mazzola's several patents on high-speed transmission techniques through twisted-pair wiring prove his technical savvy. As vice president of the workgroup business division he is responsible for all of Cisco's core routing and switching products. He is responsible for creating the end-to-end networking solutions for large corporate and institutional customers.

Don Listwin, who came to Cisco in 1991, developed Cisco's first branding campaign and consumer product strategy in 1998, the Cisco-Powered Networks promotion. Listwin also worked with the rest of the marketing team in the early 1990s to develop IBM internetworking strategies, which resulted in Cisco's 75 percent share for IBM-SNA integration (see Chapter 6). As executive vice president of the service provider and consumer lines, his duty is to build a New World communications network that will integrate data, voice, and video services. His job is to provide end-to-end networking systems for telephone companies, Internet service providers, cable companies, and wireless companies. As Cisco hurtles into the consumer market, it is also Listwin's job to develop the Cisco brand.

In early 1999, Charles Giancarlo stepped into the well-worn shoes of William Carrico and Howard Charney, his predecessors in the position of senior vice president of small/medium business. William Carrico had held the postion for a year before announcing his intent to leave and return to his beloved role as entrepreneur of start-ups. After the business reorganization of 1997, the new small/medium business division became one of Cisco's fastest-growing factions. As vice president of small/medium business Giancarlo is responsible for promoting Cisco's end-to-end Internet solutions and expanding its two-tier distribution model. His job is to provide small and midsized customers with end-to-end networking support focused on easy-to-use integrated hardware and software solutions.

Carl Redfield, Cisco's vice president of manufacturing, originally came from Digital. Redfield is a militant advocate of manufacturing and logistics via the electronic networks. And he's notorious for his optimistic and accurate assessment of Cisco's capabilities. Whenever he integrates another acquisition's product line, he'll tell the people from the new company to call off their original estimates and instead order five times as much of everything to prepare for the integration. Board member Don Valentine says that when the executives appear at board meetings a few times a year, Carl Redfield is the only one who gets a standing ovation. Redfield's main role at Cisco is to handle the logistics of who makes Cisco equipment, and where, and how. It is his role to establish and maintain the online management of the manufacturing and distribution process to ensure that products move out quickly and that inventory stockpiles never exceed minimal levels.

Douglas Allred has been Cisco's vice president of customer advocacy since 1992. His initial feat of getting the Cisco intranet and extranets up and running set a precedent for Cisco as an Internet trendsetter and established a forerunner for the Cisco Connection Online. As Cisco's vice president of customer advocacy (technical support), he is responsible for professional services, support, and services for Cisco's customers and partners worldwide. He also manages Cisco's internal information and network services.

Selby Wellman, the current senior vice president, like Chambers, began his career at IBM. He spent 15 years in various marketing and management positions. Wellman's vision of the future reflects the Cisco agenda. "Certainly, in less than five years," he said in 1999, people will be talking face to face over their PC versus the telephone. . . . You will not see Cisco too much out in the actual device because we do not make PCs or cellular phones, but when those devices have to be connected to a network, that is where Cisco enters the picture."[5]

Since 1992, Peter Solvik, Cisco's chief information officer, has gained high accolades for his achievements in creating both the CCO and Cisco's internal information systems. His creation of the CCO has earned him a reputation as an e-commerce pioneer. Solvik has been named in *CIO Magazine*'s CIO 100, *Network World*'s "50 People Who Make a Difference in Enterprise Networking," and *Inter@ctive Week*'s "25 Unsung Heroes of the Internet." He is Cisco's second most requested speaker, after Chambers.

■ KEEPING THE LEADERS

One of Cisco's amazing strengths is its ability to hold onto top managers—especially those from acquired companies. En route to creating the technology that will change the future of communications, Cisco seems also to be dead set on changing the rules for managing an organization. The business models of command-and-control organization, like that at Wang in the 1980s, is passe in contrast. In the high-tech world, where management seems to usually turn over in one or two "Internet years"—one actual calendar year for seven Internet years—Cisco seems to hold onto its executives for eternities. The foundation of Cisco's way of being is to imbue the executives—and their teams—with a strong sense of ownership of their mutual assets.

➤ Abundant (and Profitable) Stock Options

Stock options are the material manifestation of employee ownership. Everyone at Cisco has a significant personal incentive to keep Cisco's profits rising exponentially. Stock options are completely vested after four years, so that's four years of dedicated inspiration. This works particularly well when the stock keeps rising. When the options mature, Cisco gives the employee the option to buy more. And the cycle flows on, builds momentum; the people stay put, continuously inspired by the concept of a lifetime of financial freedom. "People used to say, four years, vest, and out," said Vice President of Human Resources Barbara Beck. "We haven't seen that."

Most Cisco employees have stock tickers on their terminals with up-to-the-minute information on Cisco's market performance. About 40 percent of the stock options at the company are held by nonmanagerial employees—individual contributors—whose option gains average more than $150,000. Management, naturally, is prone to have even more due to signing options and seniority. The employee security option plan at Cisco enables employees to purchase up to $25,000 in company stock each year, at 85 percent of the opening or closing price of the previous 6-month period, whichever is lower. Since Cisco's stock value seems to double every year, the deal is a steal. An average engineer granted a signing bonus of 5,000 shares of stock options in 1992 would have had nearly $3 million in stock by 1999.

➤ Enforced Team Approach

Teamwork is paramount in an organization whose size and growth rate demand it. The more decentralized Cisco's organization becomes, the more any semblance of management depends on empowered individuals working together under the benevolent command of Cisco's corporate leaders.

Chambers is notorious for instilling team spirit into the Cisco culture. He brags that he's never lost a person who reported to him. "Now I've changed a number of them," he quickly added, "but we've always been able to build, in all of my three prior companies, a team that really worked well together, that challenged each other, and was candid with each other, but one that had very, very low attrition."

Chambers is a genius at team pep talk. One chestnut proliferates in the popular biographical accounts of Chambers: Chambers and his friend, attorney Duf Sundheim, were killing some other guys in doubles tennis. According to Sundheim, their opponents were completely destroyed—so whipped that they were about to walk off the court. John went over during a break and told them about some of the good points of their playing. He pumped them up with confidence and encouragement. When Sundheim and Chambers got back on the court with them for the next round, they were entirely different players. In fact, they won the match. This is the example that Chambers would like to set internally—a "spirit of the game" approach wherein encouragement and good will empowers employees and facilitates management. Of course, such sentiments need not be applied to Lucent or Nortel.

The only downside of team spirit, the challenge that Cisco must meet, is that the emphasis on cooperation can hamper productive debate and dissent. In the beginning, Cisco veteran Barbara Beck recalls, Cisco was nearly chaotic. "John Morgridge liked very healthy discussion," she said. "The rules were: No biting, kicking, or scratching, but everything else is fair game." Chambers recalls being in shock when he first came to Cisco because he often had to get between people who were on the verge of a fistfight. Mike Volpe, Cisco's vice president of business development, remembers the team spirit of 1994 in contrast to the culture of 1999: "As we've grown we've become more PC. We're very blunt in e-mail, but person to person we're less direct and confrontational, more consensus-oriented."

➤ Encourage the Dennis Rodmans

Chambers is a big fan of basketball, and hires the Dennis Rodmans to lead the company. The Judy Estrins and

Mario Mazzolas are entrepreneurial spirits ushered to Cisco (via the acquisition of their start-up businesses) by virtue of their renegade thinking, nonconformist vision, and obvious ability to lead an industry.

"The example I use with my own leaders," Chambers told *LAN Times* in a 1996 interview, "is 'You've got to have the mavericks in Cisco. You've got to have people who challenge you.' However," he cautions, "the mavericks have to follow within reasonable bounds the course and the direction of the company. . . . Without a Jordan or a Pippin would I hire Rodman? Absolutely not." The mavericks must still work with the rest of the team—and this applies to the VPs as well as any maverick staff. Chambers switches metaphors and relates Cisco's management structure to a bunch of wild ducks. "I don't expect us to fly in formation. I just want us to go south at the same time of year, and when it's time to go north, to go north at the same time of year."

➤ Instill Diversity

Stagnation is the nemesis of the effective high-tech leader. With all the money Cisco executives make, Chambers must ensure that the environment is stimulating enough to keep people from abandoning the company for the golf ranges. "It's not that they go to competitors," Don Valentine said. "But they're distracted by other things in life. It's a constant struggle to keep it interesting to the executives." The most compelling argument is that they're among the few people building one of the world's great companies. Shortly after becoming chief technology officer, Judy Estrin told *Computer Reseller News*, "There's probably no other company in the world I would do this job for, but once you get into the role, you realize how much influence on the marketplace and the difference one can make given Cisco's leadership position." But if that sentiment wears out in the day-to-day annoyances in the years to come, Chambers wants to be proactive. His challenge is to enrich his executives' careers.

One way to combat slumping interest is to encourage Cisco executives to study other companies' cultures and decision-making processes. Cisco executives join other corporate boards in order to learn from and contribute to other businesses. Cisco management is mainly involved with companies that are also Sequoia Capital investments, due to a program that Valentine set up with Cisco. About 15 major executives at Cisco are on other boards. Judy Estrin is on the boards of directors of Federal Express, Sun Microsystems, and the Walt Disney Company. Don Listwin sits on the boards of E-TEK, Software.com, Inc., and TIBCO, all entrepreneurial companies focused on the Internet. Bill Carrico was on the board of NuvoMedia—a company that develops RocketBook electronic book devices. Doug Allred serves as a member of the boards of directors of other network services companies. "Of course if [Cisco executives] are on too many boards," Valentine hedges, "it's not in the best interest of Cisco shareholders or management, but [being on no boards] limits their development. One is certainly not too many."

➤ Reverse Fortunes

Many of the executives at Cisco, Chambers has said, have, like him, been through major crises at other high-tech firms. They've learned from those failures and have come to Cisco reformed. Gary Daichendt, who had been at Wang with Chambers, is one of many to say that one learns more through failure than through success.

Cisco is a haven compared to these executives' previous employers. And they want to keep it that way. VP Carl Redfield, a veteran of DEC, told one *Wired* reporter that "One thing that keeps Cisco healthy is as we get larger a lot of people on the executive staff have come from places that have caused their downfall. My back arches and my fur goes up when I see us going down one of those tracks, like establishing a committee to make a decision. Or making it difficult for people to get recognition, because some manager wants to grab it. Or focusing on internal competition rather than real competition. Or not being sensitive to people who are fast trackers but don't quite fit."[6]

Cisco's biggest challenge as it enters the technology wars of the next millennium is to remain flexible, an increasingly difficult task in an organization that is getting bigger and bigger. Cisco must be cohesive and team-dependent on one hand, yet progressive, adaptable, and cutting-edge on the other. Team spirit must never prevent individuals from healthy dissent. Executives must keep law and order, yet empower employees to think for themselves, bear responsibility, and resist the big-business tendency to become corporate drones. Of course, acquisitions always infuse the works with fresh blood and new ideas. But such infusions, as the American Red Cross is wont to note, can cause serious damage in an incompatible system. Cisco must act like an adolescent in a gigantic adult body, and its management must impart the same vitality and elasticity as found in a start-up. Cisco must stay versatile in its technology and, like Jordan, Pippen, and Rodman, must make swooshes by getting incompatible entities to work together. Cisco must move fast: acquire companies quickly, integrate new employees quickly, and churn out new products quickly. It must be acrobatic in its market orientation, lithe around its competitors. But its foundation—its CEO, managerial core, and culture—must be solid and steadfast.

Chapter

Giving Cisco a Voice (1998–Present)

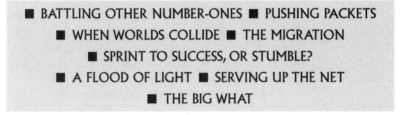

- BATTLING OTHER NUMBER-ONES ■ PUSHING PACKETS
- WHEN WORLDS COLLIDE ■ THE MIGRATION
- SPRINT TO SUCCESS, OR STUMBLE?
- A FLOOD OF LIGHT ■ SERVING UP THE NET
- THE BIG WHAT

In order for the Internet to change the way the world "works, lives, learns, and plays" (a Cisco tag line), everyone first has to be connected to a network. When connectivity, bandwidth, and flexible technologies are universally implemented and augmented, the value of the network increases. It's a rapidly accelerating cycle. Richer media, speed, and responsiveness drive users to depend more and more on the network. The more users, the more money spent, the better the network becomes. The better the network, the more popular it becomes. Cisco's future is the promise of one big, all-powerful network on which data, voice, and video will monumentally converge. Either you understand that data networking technology will determine the future or, as Chambers says, you're history.

John Chambers envisions the network as a surrogate

reality in which everything—text, image, sound—will all metamorphose into bits in a New World Network. The bits are a lingua franca—they can go everywhere, are universally translatable, and can flow easily into a variety of new gadgets that have and will emerge in the marketplace. The Net will soon be much more than a place to send e-mail and browse home pages. Digital devices of all kinds—telephones, personal digital assistants, portable sound systems, desktop computers—can translate voice into digital bits and back again through the network—even a wireless one. And all the different gadgets will require a network with increased capability for data traffic and flow as well as some sort of translator to enable them to fluently communicate with one another. Cisco, of course, intends to create much of that network. *"Are you ready?"*—Chambers ecstatically inquires—for devices that will enable the consumer to talk through the Internet from anywhere—home, office, personal computer, car, gym, boat, drive-in, or movie theater?

Chambers insists that voice calls will be free someday soon. He has hedgingly pegged 2002 as the crucial crossover point when voice transmissions over packet-switched networks (the Internet or its derivatives) will exceed voice transmissions over traditional phone lines. Traditional phone and cable companies will merge and be absorbed into oblivion. The computer and Internet companies will become the new communications industry—and Chambers wants Cisco to lead the Internet Revolution, soon to be documented in online textbooks everywhere. The revolution will replace modems with cable-TV boxes, DSL connections, and wireless connections. Online psychics will be able to tell fortunes on demand in real time. Students will get remote access to the world's best universities. Businesses in third-world countries will be able to sell to customers worldwide, bringing the rewards of the Internet to entrepeneurial people across the globe. Everything will be much faster and will cost about the price of a local phone call today.

With boosted brand recognition, ubiquitous advertising, and an undercurrent of new technology that will replace traditional phone lines, Cisco will have not only a public face, but a voice with which to proclaim itself remarkable.

■ BATTLING OTHER NUMBER-ONES

In many ways, 1999 marked the coming out of Cisco. First, it won the data-networking race. Cisco's market share in all of its product areas rose, dwarfing its competitors in its core markets. The datacom industry was shaken up. Some of its competitors were bought out. Others, like IBM, just threw in the towel. The independent survivors live in a Cisco-dominated world, selling low-margin or niche products while Cisco continues to enjoy high profits and rapid growth.

Second, Cisco was accepted into the telecommunications world. The industry journal *Telecommunications Online* grouped Cisco with Lucent, Nortel, Alcatel, Siemens, and Ericsson, calling them the Big Six telecom equipment manufacturers, though Cisco's revenues and headcount were dwarfed by the others. When Chambers refocused Cisco from selling equipment to companies and ISPs for data networks to creating a network that converges data, sound, and video and selling it to phone companies, he entered a whole new league.

Cisco has a formidable track record to maintain: Out of 20 product areas, it's number 1 in market share in 16 and number 2 in 4. Abiding by the golden rule—be number one or number two in an industry or don't be in it—Cisco has a lot of pressure.

Cisco's greatest competitors are now the dominant (and, in Cisco's slanted view, Old World) U.S. telecom equipment providers, Lucent and Nortel. The two telephony giants are definitely more formidable rivals than

Cisco has ever known in the New World of computer networks. In 1999, Nortel was twice as big as Cisco in revenues. Lucent was three times as big. In fact, Lucent and Nortel executives publicly seethe over Cisco's ability to present itself as a telecom leader, when they are many times its size. And Cisco must now court the companies that have been exclusively these giants' sweethearts—service providers like WorldCom, AT&T, and Sprint. In the past, Cisco sold networks directly to corporations. Now it must sell much bigger networks to telco giants to serve millions of customers. Lucent CEO Richard McGinn declared, "It will take Cisco time, effort, and substantial investment in distribution to address the far-flung needs of communications enterprises."[1]

➤ Lucent

Lucent grew out of Bell Labs, AT&T's research lab, which has been a pioneer in many fields of technology. Like Bell Labs, which it has retained, Lucent is still based in Murray Hills, New Jersey. Lucent is a leader in fiber-optic technology, a crucial component of the networks of the future. It clearly outclasses Cisco in this area.

Lucent absorbed a top datacom player when it acquired Ascend for $24 billion in early 1999. Prior to the acquisition, Lucent was late to move toward data convergence and the Internet. It had been hampered by tax laws that made a large acquisition prohibitive until late 1998. Ascend, with $1 billion in revenues, had been cutting into sales of Lucent's circuit switches with its own switches for ATM. Rather than take a year to catch up, Lucent decided to purchase the company. Over 90 percent of Ascend's employees stayed on after the purchase. Although Lucent (located in Murray Hills, New Jersey) has a much more buttoned-down culture than the start-up Ascend (located in California and Massachusetts), Lucent gave Ascend enough autonomy to continue to act like a small company and conduct business as usual. Lucent isn't acting like a big dinosaur that is willing to roll over and die. The people at Ascend are developing the same thing Cisco is: ways to transmit voice data over the Net. Between 1996 and 1999, Lucent also purchased 11 data networking companies, including SpecTran Corp, maker of fiber-optic products; Maszix, a customer service software maker; and network designer International Network Services.

On top of it all, as Lucent likes to advertise, it has an advantage over its rivals by having in its stables a 25,000-employee idea factory for research and development, the famed Bell Labs. Bell Labs is literally where telephony began more than 100 years ago. Its engineers have a research budget that is correlated directly to Lucent's earnings. For every 10 percent increase in Lucent's revenues, the research budget also rises 10 percent. And so far, Bell Labs has been extraordinarily productive, churning out three patents a day. However, David House, Nortel's president, is skeptical. Although Lucent has a lot of good telephony capability, he says, "It's just not quite as good as they think it is. They believe their own advertising."[2] Though Lucent's telephony equipment is the market leader, Lucent doesn't have all the answers to every future problem.

While Lucent's legacy base is a blessing in that it allows the company to attempt a graceful evolution, it can also be a curse. Lucent's 5ESS switches, which connect more than 110 million telephone lines to AT&T's network, may prove to be a huge albatross. No matter what developments Lucent pursues or whatever acquisitions it attains, Lucent is obligated to take into account the costly, proprietary, house-sized 5ESS switches. Some critics suggest that Lucent is particularly wedded to ATM, because that technology works well with legacy systems. When and if newer telecom companies without a lot of old equipment make the transition to IP without ATM, Lucent may not be as sure-footed. When IPG Communications of Englewood, Colorado, decided to develop voice services over an IP-only network, it asked network companies to demonstrate their equipment. Lucent's didn't impress IPG, and Cisco won the $5 million contract.

➤ Nortel Networks

Nortel, based in Canada, has impressive expertise and market share in equipment for wireless and satellite communications, another crucial technology of the future. Cisco, while making some forays into wireless, has no satellite presence at all.

In the summer of 1998, Nortel purchased Bay Networks, one of Cisco's closest competitors, for $9.1 billion. Northern Telecommunications officially changed its name to Nortel Networks with the acquisition, emphasizing its shift toward data networks. Nortel itself had been a growing contender in interoffice networking, with $1 billion in annual revenues, but it lacked data communications expertise. It acquired Bay to become a viable competitor with Cisco. The acquisition was a boon to Bay as well. After its mighty NIA days, it struggled when Wellfleet and Synoptics merged, missed its promised delivery dates, and, in Chambers's words, "lost track of the customer." Under new CEO Dave House, lured from Intel, Bay had been striving to reconstitute its old image as a networking leader. It acquired another switching company and touted a new strategy—next-generation networking, based on switched IP networks, to help traditional phone carriers migrate from circuit-based networks to Internet-based ones. It seemed to be on the mend when Nortel acquired it as a wholly owned subsidiary.

Backed up by Nortel, Bay can develop its portfolio of networking products and have them implemented by a well-established service provider. Nortel likewise benefits from the acquisition by gaining instant legitimacy in the data networking arena. It also acquired Bay's distribution channels and customer lists, and now is developing technology that Lucent and Cisco are touching: technology that enables voice calls to carry over cable-TV lines, a small yet potentially lucrative market. Although still behind Lucent in the telecom industry, Nortel has positioned itself to be a one-stop provider of data networks and a significant contender against Cisco.

Lagging behind Lucent and Nortel are the European telecom providers: Alcatel, Siemens, and Ericsson. Hampered by the slow-moving networking market in Europe, these companies are making numerous acquisitions in the U.S. in an attempt to stay competitive.

➤ Alcatel

Cisco and Alcatel, based in France, go way back, especially if one is counting in Internet years. In 1993, Alcatel, then the world's largest supplier of telecommunications equipment, signed an original equipment manufcturer (OEM) agreement with Cisco—Alcatel would offer Cisco products as its preferred partner for router equipment. In 1997, they agreed to resell certain equipment for each other, but then decided they were going to be competing in important areas. In 1999, Alcatel, then the world's fourth largest telecom company, acquired two U.S.-based data networking companies, Xylan and Assured Access, that would compete with Cisco in the voice convergence arena. Rumors that the alliance was dying abounded. Thierry Labbe, executive chairman of Cisco France, denied the allegation. However, Serge Tchurik, Alcatel's chairman and CEO, forthrightly deemed Cisco a competitor.

➤ Siemens

Telecommunications and computer giant Siemens, based in Germany, made several critical U.S.-based acquisitions in order to position itself in the data convergence industry. It had been working toward this goal in the mid- to late 1990s, beginning with its middecade alliances with 3Com and Newbridge Networks. In 1999, Siemens purchased Unisphere (a data and IP networking company), Argon Networks (a hybrid IP router/ATM switch maker), and Castle Networks (a bridge circuit–switched and packet-switched systems business). Unisphere, like the other Siemens acquisitions, targets service providers and local exchange carriers, with the goal of being the end-to-end supplier of communication solutions. Argon, at the time of purchase, already boasted a 20- to 160-gigabit IP router. Castle is the self-proclaimed voice and data convergence specialist for public network providers, offering high-performance IP routing with ATM switching. For all intents and purposes, Siemens seems to be moving into carrier-class IP and ATM switching companies, while the other Big Six companies, primarily Alcatel and Lucent, have been vying for the corporate data networking market. And these end-of-the millennium purchases are only the beginning, Siemens says, having put aside $1 billion for acquisitions in the IP networking arena. The only blatant disadvantage Siemens has relative to its U.S. competitors is that Siemens will have to pay cash for its new companies, unlike companies on the U.S. stock exchange that can acquire larger companies with stock.

➤ Ericsson

Then there's Ericsson, based in Sweden, and Nokia, based in Finland, leaders in mobile communications. Ericsson and Nokia are forging ahead in a market that is Cisco's particular Achilles' heel: wireless communications. In 1995, Cisco and Nokia formed a strategic alliance to provide ATM-based voice and data networking solutions. In 1996, Cisco and Ericsson collaborated on the development of wireless Internet services, but this market has grown slowly for Cisco. Nokia and Ericsson have thrived in wireless communications. In fact, over 43 percent of Ericsson's revenues come from the manufacture and sale of wireless infrastructure equipment; 25 percent come from the sale of cell phones. Its penetration of the data convergence market, however, is rather weak, unless it can find and acquire a promising start-up. One promising development for Ericsson was the 1999 acquisition of Advanced Computer Communications, a remote access concentrator maker. Nokia, for its part, acquired Ipsilon, a networking infrastructure provider once heralded as a Cisco killer, for $120 million.

➤ The Start-ups

Chambers continues to regard the small players as legitimate competition. "I have a list of a dozen little companies that I'm tracking very closely," he said. "Guys who start from a fresh sheet of paper have an enormous advantage technologically. We have to carefully integrate new capabilities into our existing product lines, and that is tougher, They keep us on our toes."[3] There are a lot of hot little start-ups, such as Juniper Networks, Avici Systems, and Pluris, some of which are not quite autonomous. Lucent is one of Juniper's investors. Nortel owns 20 percent of Avici.

Way back at its inception in early 1996, the tiny start-up Juniper announced that it would set out to produce a new generation of Internet routing devices that would replace Cisco's routers and switches. Over the following years, Juniper amassed a total of $62 million in funding from companies such as Lucent, 3Com, IBM, Nortel, Ericsson, Siemens, UUNet, and a few venture capitalists—all of whom are eager to usurp Cisco. Many of them have product distribution rights as well as the right to integrate Juniper's technology into their product lines and services. Avici, fueled with an initial $16 million in venture funding, gained another $39 million when Nortel purchased its stake, and then won $17 million more in a second round of finding. With a spectacular IPO in 1999, Juniper became one of the hottest companies on the stock market.

Although much of the technology these companies are developing is still experimental and extremely costly, their sponsors are placing bets now for the future. Some of the start-ups are promising terabit speeds by virtue of more clever engineering. Some want to replace Cisco's router software (its IOS) with special silicon chips—application-specific integrated circuits (ASICS)—that can move data faster. Others are working on the hybrid technologies, with higher-speed ATM devices running zippy IP. All these companies are stuck with having to deliver products that are compatible with Cisco's infrastructure, much as everyone has to take into account the legacy telephone system.

Cisco's advantage over its rivals is its history as a data networker and a builder of the Internet infrastructure. It has a dominant market share in routers and is the leader in local-area network and wide-area network switches. The IP- and ATM-based networks that Cisco produces are beginning to be effective conveyors of voice. Chambers crows constantly about using Cisco's IP network to save long-distance charges. Chambers fails to mention, of course, that Cisco has struggled to develop a network that is reliable, robust, and cheap enough to sell on the open market.

■ PUSHING PACKETS

Everyone in both the data communications and telecommunications industries has been able to see the writing on the wall for years: The traditional circuit switching of phone networks is going to be replaced by packet switching. The critical difference between packet-switched networks and the existing circuit-switched ones is that the latter uses a dedicated line. A traditional phone call establishes a circuit for the duration of the call, which is like freeing an entire highway lane for a single car. Such a system guarantees excellent quality: clear sound, few disruptions, and no unexpected hang-ups. Creating a single, dedicated highway lane for every car on the road would be wasteful—as Chambers puts it, "You don't need 5,000 highways across North America." Traditional telephony is wasteful and expensive. And communications are becoming more and more demanding.

The solution is to chop up telephone calls—to break voice transmissions, like all other data on the Internet, into IP packets and send them over the Net. Voice data packets will jostle around with other packets and find the most efficient route over the Net. On the other end of the line, wherever that may be, the packets will reassemble themselves into analog words understandable to the human ear.

Pundits and companies agree that by 2005, give or take a few years, all networks will be pure IP, using one intelligent packet technology to carry data, voice, and video. By that time, hardware and software advances will allow a complex soup of services to be handled at the needed speed.

Vast engineering resources are being brought to bear to make this idea a reality. But it's not an easy switch. For one thing, the billions of dollars worth of existing phone gear already in place is not going to be immediately dismantled and dumped into the landfill. It still works. Moreover, traditional data networks, the kind that made Cisco a superstar, including the Internet, carry packets that all look alike. A data network that can reliably handle voice and video, on the other hand, has to be able to prioritize data packets and shove those with the highest priority through first. The network needs to ensure that a glut of e-mail jokes doesn't swamp a crucial business call or a scheduled television show.

The Internet industry in which Cisco thrives is built on a tradition of rapid development at the expense of reliability and tolerance of flaws that would be insufferable in the phone industry. There are, in fact, two problems here. One is the overall unreliability of computer equipment. Computers, especially those under heavy loads, fry and die every day. The software is just as bad, crashing left and right. Whole sections of the Internet slow to a crawl or drop off the map regularly. These industries have focused on adding new power and new features at lightning speed, rather than freezing their designs at a particular level and concentrating on making them more reliable. Phone equipment, by comparison, has been around for over a century, enabling it to become highly reliable. Phone equipment is exceedingly redundant; it's almost impossible to kill a phone switch. When people pick up a receiver, they don't hear white noise or dead silence; they get a dial tone.

The second problem is a technical difference. The Internet runs under a best-effort regime—there's no guarantee of reliability. An e-mail may take two minutes to reach its destination, or disappear entirely and never arrive. In telephony, even a split-second delay would ripple the fluidity of a conversation. The reliability of phone connections are rigidly laid out in quality-of-service (QoS) standards. A system following the QoS standards ensures clean, uninterrupted phone conversations. So Cisco has a long way to go to hone its technology to the extent that it can be number one in a voice communications network. Cisco has to bring reliability to datacom equipment and performance. But, then again, so do its competitors.

Moreover, the copper wire that used to run all data and telephone networks won't cut it for much longer. The convergent network of tomorrow requires pipes of fiberglass literally flashing light to handle unbelievably large volumes of voice, video, and textual data. Electrical digital pulses are converted to light pulses and are transmitted through fiber-optic cables. You can cram orders of magnitude more light pulses onto fiber than you can electrical pulses onto wire. The fiber-optic network will also require new equipment—which Cisco likes to call routers, but this is a new breed—that will internetwork the fiberglass at fiber-optic speeds.

■ WHEN WORLDS COLLIDE

"It's a battle of New World versus Old World," as Chambers describes the territorial conflicts to create the telecommunications infrastructure of the twenty-first century. *Wired* magazine labeled it the battle of the Netheads versus the Bellheads. The way Chambers sees it, it will be Cisco that will convert the Old World into the New, in a manner not unlike bringing the Dark Ages into the Enlightenment. Legacy systems in the telecom industry will have to be integrated into new, digital, Internet-based transmission protocols. Everything, from lines to equipment to software, will have to be replaced. But, Chambers asserts, the changeover will come with big savings for customers. His pitch (based on a study by Renaissance World Wide, an independent market researcher), is that a large company would get a minimum return on investment of 161 percent over 3 years by moving all data, voice, and video to a singular, unified network. In turn, the $500-billion-a-year telecom industry promises expanding returns for whatever companies corner the data convergence market in the new millennium.

There's too much hype, cried a Forrester Research study released in August 1998. The report declared that networks that converge voice and data won't become ubiquitous because they'll actually come with minimal cost savings, will introduce more network complexities, and will suffer from the truculence of local phone companies. Combining everything onto one platform won't be simpler, it said. One Forrester analyst asserted that no matter how well it is engineered, voice over the Internet cannot get any better and, as a result, "multiple networks will live on forever." Or, at least, 10 years will pass before any phone company feels the impetus to upgrade its infrastructure to a converged voice and data platform.

Their pessimism is increasingly a shout in the woods.

Cisco has much higher expectations than Forrester and much more accelerated projections. So do its rivals. Though there has been too much hype, in five years' time the world is going to be a very different place—at least in the United States. The United States is the battleground, and is at least two, maybe five, years ahead of Europe in establishing convergent networks. This change is going to be a whirlwind.

Cisco is doggedly trying to gain entry to a telecom culture in which executives have rubbed each other's shoulders for decades. Chambers and Don Listwin now make a habit of regularly meeting with the heads of the world's 100 biggest phone companies to discuss the future. Cisco had less than 1 percent of the worldwide phone equipment market in 1999, but has sold gear to most phone carriers for their Internet services. What Cisco would really like to initiate through these meetings are big network overhauls—the wholesale conversion of plain old telephone lines into electronic pipelines. Which can be a problem: Cisco is basically asking telecom service providers to throw out all their old equipment—gear they've invested hundreds of billions in over the years. Lucent and Nortel are merely telling their long-time pals that they'll provide a "graceful evolution"—eventually ending up with the same electronic pipelines. These old companies know the technology that's worked for 100 years, and they have one leg up on developing a means to upgrade gradually.

Following his previous strategy of partnering with rival companies when he can see an advantage in making their equipment work together rather than entering each other's markets, Chambers proposed partnerships with Lucent and Nortel. Both spurned Chambers's advances, claiming that his proposal left Cisco with the choicest cut of the market: the primary equipment for transmitting data. Lucent and Nortel would have been left with the digital corporate phone business. These companies resent Cisco's huge market capitalization and brazen attitude. Any initiatory talks with Nortel ended promptly when Nortel acquired Bay Networks in May 1998. One month later, Lucent sued Cisco for eight patent infringements related to data networking. Kevin Kennedy, senior vice president of Cisco's service provider business, asserted that Lucent's action was a marketing tactic designed to slow down industry leaders. Other rumors circulated that Lucent had offered to acquire Cisco and, after Chambers declined, sued out of spite. Cisco spun around and countersued Lucent in August of the same year for six patent infringement allegations. Meanwhile, the Federal Trade Commission launched an investigation of Cisco's advances to Lucent and Nortel. The Feds were questioning whether Chambers's proposal constituted collusion—dividing up the market to avoid competition. Federal scrutiny is tougher on companies like Cisco that approach monopoly status. Cisco was having a rough time of it in 1998, and its stock suffered, plunging 32 percent from its $100 billion high.

Everything settled down a year later. In June 1999, both Cisco and Lucent agreed to settle the lawsuits by cross-licensing technology, which, although not a partnership, enabled both companies to continue to forge ahead on their respective paths. In August, the FTC dropped its investigation, perhaps because the Feds concluded the Cisco's strength in datacom didn't mean that much in the world of telecom. Cisco's stock was back to its old tricks, reaching new, dizzying highs.

Cisco's advantage in this struggle is that cobbling together disparate systems into a coherent network is what it does best. Certainly, Lucent and Nortel and the others face the same challenges that Cisco does in developing a network that will converge voice, video, and data reliably. Lucent, Nortel, and Alcatel are relative neophytes in mastering the art of transferring digital data. Cisco claimed to be as much as 18 months (a huge lead in Internet time) ahead of its competitors at the end of 1999. Cisco's rivals are buying those skills by acquiring networking companies, much as Cisco itself moves into new businesses by acquiring smaller companies in the desired arena. The New and Old Worlds are melding.

■ THE MIGRATION

The battle over the future of phone networks began in the early 1990s. Everyone wanted to move from circuit switching to packet switching, but how? The debate was popularly framed as being between the Old World telcos in support of ATM and the New World datacom kids in support of IP, pure packets all the way, with the complex circuit-packet hybrid proponents in the middle. The debate still goes on. Neither of the technologies was ready for the demands of the telephone networks at the time; in fact, by the year 2000, they were still only getting there. Moreover, the situation is simply more complicated than a simple either/or choice. IP and ATM aren't exclusive technologies. An IP network can be built on ATM equipment.

Pure IP networks are the way of the future. But companies have to sell products that work today, not tomorrow. Though IP proponents mock ATM for its complexity, they've spent years trying desperately to enable IP to match ATM's ability to handle connections with only modest gains: By May 1999, Cisco, the number-one player in VoIP, could only muster a VoIP network of 150 users. Many of the gains have come at the price of adding layer upon layer of complexity to IP, so that it's now carrying a lot of ATM's baggage.

Though ATM has been vilified as yesterday's technology, it works pretty well. Even the professedly pure IP telcos like Qwest and Level 3 Communications have quite a few ATM switches in their networks. Cisco, which pushed IP harder than anyone else when it began its move into the carrier market, has listened to the wind and backed away from acting like an IP zealot, and now offers combined IP and ATM solutions. Lucent came from the other side and introduced its own IP on ATM switches in the summer of 1999.

Cisco, Nortel, Lucent, and the other players are now working on developing some sort of transition technology that will carry legacy systems into the age of the new networks. Cisco's only possible winning strategy is to replace the entire system as quickly as possible. Although Cisco has revamped and reinforced its ATM product lines with the acquisition of StrataCom, many analysts give Lucent (owner of Ascend) first place in that arena. When Lucent acquired Ascend, it inherited the majority of ATM switches installed in U.S. service providers' systems.

Cisco, to compete effectively in the convergence market of 1999, went back to the playbook and went on an acquisition spree. It acquired seven companies by the end of the summer of 1999, the first four in the month of April. In an attempt to catch up to Lucent in the field of voice on ATM, a market it had disdained, Cisco snapped up Fibex and Sentient. GeoTel and Amteva's software improved its phone services. GeoTel, of Lowell, Massachusetts, was a big acquisition at $2 billion. Its CEO, John Thibault, became senior vice president of the applications technology group, overseeing the GeoTel and Amteva operations, as well as the September acquisition of WebLine Communications, with its smart online customer management software. The June acquisition of TransMedia complemented Fibex and Sentient's ATM package. Calista, based in Chalfont Saint Peter, England, gave Cisco the ability to emulate traditional private phone systems on an IP network; it was acquired for $55 million in August.

By September, Cisco was able to connect small IP voice, video, and data networks to traditional phone networks, but didn't have enough firepower to push the reliable legacy systems into obsolescence. Cisco's next declared strategy was to replace the private phone networks used in office buildings, and then the public networks, with an entirely IP-based network. Cisco still has a long way to go before it succeeds.

■ SPRINT TO SUCCESS, OR STUMBLE?

In June 1998, Sprint announced it would build the world's first voice, video, and data network—and Cisco won the contract to supply the equipment. Chambers scored a major coup by snatching the contract away from Nortel, Sprint's original choice. $2 billion after Cisco signed on, the two companies had produced the Sprint integrated on-demand network (ION), intended to provide the customer with as much network capacity as necessary for combined video, voice, and data service. This is Chambers's vision of the future, and Sprint is building it. At ION's grand debut ceremony at the Richard Rodgers Theater in New York, Sprint Chairman and CEO Bill Esrey deemed ION a "revolutionary new set of technological advancements."

People in the small community of Gardner, Missouri, where ION is being tested, plug all their telephone lines, televisions, fax machines, computers, and other devices into a VCR-sized box. The box routes all the different sorts of data through a single line via Cisco's IP-over-ATM network at unlimited bandwidth and high speeds. Citizens of Gardner can now download movies and videoconference with their grandchildren for the price of a regular long-distance call—all part of Chambers's vision for the New World Network.

But not everything has been so cheerful for Sprint's revolutionary endeavor. ION has fallen behind schedule. ION was originally due to debut in 27 U.S. cities by December 1999. In April 1999, ION's expected debut was pushed back to 2000. The home market for the $200 VCR-sized box is not promising: Customers do not have a record of being fabulously eager to purchase add-on boxes from phone companies. If the market for cable modems is any indication of the interest in a broadband integrated network in the home, trouble looms, because the majority of customers aren't interested. Notoriously pokey local phone companies will be slow to lease direct connections to customers. Beta testers have been reticent with the press. Ernst & Young, after asserting that ION provides very high-potential technology, admitted that there were "network issues that needed to be worked through." Sprint has promoted ION as the network of the future, but the future of networking is pure IP, which ION is not.[4]

■ A FLOOD OF LIGHT

The future of networking is also fiber optics. Nineteen ninety-nine brought the optical deluge. Cisco has made a concerted effort to woo young telcos, cutting a big deal with Qwest in June, while building up its optical networking abilities. Cisco spent $8 billion to acquire the technology it needed. Most of that money went to Cerent, in an earth-shattering $6.9-billion deal for a 275-employee company with about $15 million in annual revenues. Needless to say, Chambers surprised a lot of people with this move.

In the last few years, new telecommunications carriers like Qwest, Level 3 Communications, and Williams have sprung onto the scene with next-generation optical networks. Cisco has worked closely with Qwest to advance both companies' fortunes. Qwest began at the end of 1996 from nothing but an AT&T executive with a grudge and a man with a railroad—Joseph Naccio, the CEO of Qwest, who left AT&T after being passed over for the chairmanship in 1996, and Philip Anschutz, the majority owner of Qwest, who sold the Southern Pacific Railroad to Union Pacific in 1996 but retained the rights of way. Over the next two years, Qwest laid down a huge fiber-optic network alongside the tracks, one that dwarfed those of the traditional telcos, AT&T, MCI, and Sprint. And Qwest didn't even have to pay for it. Companies such as WorldCom (which now owns Sprint and MCI), GTE, and Frontier Communications paid Qwest to lay down cable for them at the same time. By 1999, Qwest's network, with the capacity to carry all the traffic in the world many times over, was ready to go. Qwest placed its bets on an IP network, and looked to Cisco for help. On June 17, 1999, Cisco and Qwest announced that Qwest would use Cisco equipment to handle 80 percent of its traffic. Qwest, in its voracious way, also announced that it was making a hostile takeover of US West, another company that had worked closely with Cisco.

At the time, Cisco was way behind Lucent and upstarts like Juniper Networks and Redback Networks in optical internetworking. So on June 29, Cisco paid $435 million to acquire StratumOne Communications for its hardware expertise, plumping Graeme Fraser's optical internetworking business unit to 450 people.

Chambers spent some serious capital for Cerent and Monterey Networks, optical transport start-ups, on August 26. Cisco had already made minority investments in both privately held companies. While Monterey Networks, based in Texas, went for a reasonable $500 million (less than $5 million per employee), Cerent cost $6.9 billion, about $25 million per employee. The *Wall Street Journal* reported that Chambers initially choked on the huge price. In fact, some reports on the deal resembled those on the Crescendo acquisition of six years before, expressing shock at the money Cisco was spending on such a small company—but the numbers added up, according to Chambers. In first half of 1999, Cerent had only $10 million in sales. Cerent anticipated sales of $300 million over the following 12 months, which would give a purchase price of about 23 times sales, in line with Cisco's financial structure. Also, Cerent was planning to go public. Similar companies, Juniper Networks and Redback Networks, were trading at astronomical values—$11 billion and $6 billion, respectively. Finally, with Cerent and Monterey, Cisco could finally play in the emerging optical transport market, which analysts expected to grow to about $15 billion by 2002. Looking at it that way, $7.4 billion for 400 people might not be a bad deal for Cisco, a company valued at around $200 billion. John Chambers just has to hope that

Cerent will enjoy 3,000 percent sales growth in 1 year, which would be absolutely stupendous.

■ SERVING UP THE NET

Chambers is expanding Cisco in all directions from its roots in large corporate data networking. Along with its massive push into telecommunications, Cisco has established several initiatives to extend its reach into small business and small outposts of large businesses.

Virtual private networking is a method of using the Internet as a private network, instead of actually building a private network. This is done by encrypting the data passed over the Internet so that no one else can read it. Using encrypted channels on the public Internet, virtual private networks mimic a dedicated network at a fraction of the cost. It's certainly to Cisco's advantage to push this solution, as it requires more complex and expensive equipment than do traditional wide-area networks.

Small and medium businesses offer a special challenge to Cisco. Chambers wants to tap the market, but those businesses mainly purchase inexpensive, low-margin equipment, something he hates. So Cisco is mainly selling them services, rather than equipment. The Cisco Resource Network, begun in April 1999, allows vendors (consultants, resellers, and hardware and software manufacturers) to offer their products to small and medium businesses in packages of Cisco's pet projects, such as multiservice IP networks or virtual private networks. Cisco wants to make the Resource Network the one destination for all business management needs, from manufacturing to e-commerce to human resources.

These softwarecentric initiatives are finally making Cisco's IOS more than a marketing ploy. Combining numerous recent acquisitions and in-house research and development, Cisco has begun to offer a cornucopia of networking software abilities, from a unified phone and e-mail mailbox to e-commerce and customer support packages. There's one specter looming: Anyone who moves into software butts up against Microsoft. Chambers makes playing nice with Bill Gates a top priority. Cisco's software packages run on Windows. Cisco has stuck with Microsoft's Active Directory project since late 1996, though it is more than two years behind schedule and is playing catch-up to competitive offerings from Novell. Chambers has been forced to appease both Microsoft and Novell to keep everyone happy, an unenviable task. Cisco will continue its move into consumer software and services, and Microsoft will continue its move into the world of internetworking. The Cisco-Microsoft relationship bears watching. It could degrade and become very ugly.

■ THE BIG WHAT

John Chambers is sailing into the future, sailing toward the big . . . what? His vision of a common universal network is shared by many, but there's still a lot of disagreement. The networked future is obviously not just the product of punditry and CEO bombast. The World Wide Web has grown as fast in 5 years as the phone networks did in 30. Current trends point to the speedy dominance of data networks—in other words, the Internet. In October 1998, analysts predicted that data traffic would surpass voice traffic in the United States by 2000. The Yankee Group predicts that 70 percent of all traffic will be data by 2004. The rest of the world will follow—Europe behind North America (except in wireless), and Japan still further behind (Japan's weak economy and cultural bias have stymied the growth of networking and IT there).

The biggest unresolved problem, perhaps the one that will determine which company will come out on top, revolves around money and service. John Chambers has baldly stated, repeatedly, "Voice will be free." That monthly phone bills can be calculated in this age of competing phone networks, carriers, and technologies is something of a miracle. The reason phone networks work reliably is that connections can be separately identified and handled—and billed. That's the quality-of-service deal. Free long-distance over the Internet is a temporary phenomenon of the Internet's inability to distinguish packets.

Chambers gets great press for saying voice will be free in the future, and he may be right, but he's purposely confusing the issue. Lucent and Nortel have great strength in the field of telephony services, like call processing and billing. Cisco doesn't. There is no way that reliable connections will come without a price. Prioritized high-bandwith connections, such as real-time video, will cost more than e-mail or a low-quality phone connection. A crude analogue of this scenario is clear today. Want to download the latest *Star Wars* trailer in a minute? You need a superexpensive connection to the Internet. Willing to wait an hour? That'll cost just $9.95 a month. In the future, everyone will have similar capacity, and will be able to choose the level of speed and quality they're willing to pay for with each connection they make.

As the networks grow, they're becoming faster, cheaper, and more widely available. In a few years, transmission speeds across the entire network will be able to handle video. A fulltime connection to the Net will be cheap enough for the average household. More and more devices will be able to connect to networks. These simple extrapolations from recent history lead to no end of grandiose posturing by people like John Chambers, Jeff Bezos, and Bill Gates.

A nexus of contention is the last mile, connecting the super-fat-fiber network backbone to the fast local networks of the home and office. It's the bottleneck today, and will continue to be so in the near future. The dream is to eliminate all data friction. There are some big fans of the all-optical network, of totally replacing wire and electricity with fiber and light. The backbone already is moving to all fiber optic, and the phone backbone is already all fiber optic. But installing fiber lines to every street corner of Anytown, U.S.A., is a daunting proposition. David House believes the solution is a wireless connection. "There is not an advantage to using that wire, and you don't need to use it for the last 100 feet. So we'll save the cost of the end of the tree, and we'll put in wireless stations around our buildings and we'll be able to operate within our structure in a wireless environment." Wireless networking is just beginning to come on strong, but it's still a lot less reliable than using wire. There is also a question of security. It's much harder to interfere with or snoop on a signal traveling through a wire compared to one traveling over the air, a problem wireless proponents have to address.

The universal wireless network and the smart home are bolder predictions. As networks converge to operate on common protocols, distinctions blur. In the universal wireless network, you can use your phone or device on the corporate network at the office, on the service provider network outdoors, and on your own network at home. Though different entities pay for and maintain each network, the transition between them is invisible. The idea of a smart home—with a computer running all aspects of a house—has been around for a while, and has failed to catch on as quickly as was predicted. But with a ubiquitous network, a smart house makes sense—the objects in the house could cooperate with each other and with the outside world. The refrigerator, cupboards, and trash could work together to replenish food supplies by reordering from the supermarket automatically. (There are already people doing this.) John Chambers has his player piano hooked to the Net—it downloads and plays music. There's no technical reason that every household object couldn't be similarly connected to an appropriate Net-based service.

The funny thing about the strange and exciting possibilities that Chambers and others detail is that this is old news. The scientists and engineers who designed and built the Net envisioned a ubiquitous network aiding humans in their daily lives back in the 1960s. In his 1960 paper, "Man-Computer Symbiosis," networking seer (and behavioral psychologist by training) J. C. R. Licklider forsaw the integration of the functions of libraries with symbiotic computing over an "intergalactic network," the promise that Chambers harps on today. The early pioneers have been frustrated that the future has been so evident but so hard to reach, but revolutions take time. The vision is clear, because the potential of the network lies not in technology but in people. Networks erase distance and blur hierarchies. The Web is already engendering great social and economic upheavals, rewriting the rules of wealth generation. If the Internet evolves into a global network that everyone, not just the wealthy and the techno-elite, can share, then Chambers's Internet Revolution may indeed occur.

The world Cisco faces at the turn of the millennium parallels the one that first propelled Cisco to success. It's a world of incompatible protocols, preventing people from communicating. This time, people want their phones, televisions, and computers to talk to each other. Cisco has moved to provide the consumer product equivalent of its original multiprotocol router—the media gateway, which can connect phone networks of various types to the various data networks. With any luck for Cisco, history will repeat itself. Cisco's multiprotocol routers led the first wave of network convergence that resulted in the World Wide Web, and Chambers intends for Cisco to lead the second wave, as well. Now Cisco is armed with more than black boxes; it also sells the ideas behind its success. Of course, history could repeat itself in another way: A small, innovative company could come along—unburdened by hype, huge product lines, and an organization of thousands—to become the *next* company of the future.

Notes

CHAPTER 1

1. Stephen Segaller, *Nerds 2.0.1* (New York: TV Books, 1998), p. 242.
2. Joseph Nocera, "Cooking with Cisco: What Does It Take to Keep a Hot Stock Sizzling?" *Fortune,* 25 December 1995, p. 35.
3. Robert X. Cringely, "High Tech Wealth," *Forbes,* 7 July 1997, www.forbes.com/forbes/97/0707/6001296a.htm.

CHAPTER 2

1. David Brousell, "Cisco Chief Outlines Ways Companies Embrace a Networked Business Model," http://info.comdex.com, 1 November 1997.

CHAPTER 3

1. Neil Stephenson, *Snow Crash* (New York: Spectra Books, 1993).
2. Geoff Baum, "Cisco's CEO: John Chambers," *Forbes ASAP,* 23 February 1998, www.forbes.com/asap/98/0223/052.htm.

3. Andy Reinhardt, "Meet Cisco's Mr. Internet," *Business Week,* 13 September 1999, www.businessweek.com/reprints/99-37/ b3646001.htm.

4. Leonard Heymann, Jeremiah Caron, and Michelle Rae McLean, "Q&A: The Star Chambers, *LAN Times,* July 1996, www.lantimes.com/96jul/607a001b.html.

5. Heymann.

6. Heymann.

7. Baum.

8. Heymann.

CHAPTER 4

1. Harvard Business School case study, Nolan, Cisco Systems, Inc. 10/13/98.

2. Glenn Rifkin, "Growth by Acquisition: The Case of Cisco Systems," *Thought Leaders* (Booz, Allen, and Hamilton), Second Quarter 1997, www.strategy-business.com/thoughtleaders/97209/ page4.html.

3. Hal Plotkin, "Cisco's Secret: Entrepreneurs Sell Out, Stay Put," *Inc.,* March 1997, www.inc.com/articles/details/0,6378,AGD10_ ART1180_CNT56_SUB26,00.html.

4. Charles O'Reilly, *Cisco Systems: The Acquisition of Technology Is the Acquisition of People,* study no. HR-10, Graduate School of Business, Stanford University, 27 October 1998: 5.

5. AT&T, "Cisco, StrataCom, AT&T Share ATM Vision and Development Plans," 12 January 1993, www.att.com/press/0193/ 930112.bsb.html.

6. Eric Nee, "Interview with John Chambers," *Upside,* 30 June 1996.

7. Kelly Jackson-Higgins, "Cisco's $4.5 billion gamble—Will StrataCom products, culture fit in?" *Communications Week* iss. 625 26 August, 1996. http://www.techweb.com/se/directlink .cgi?CWK19960826S0002.

8. Jackson-Higgins.

9. Eric Lach, "Cisco Pulls Plug on LightStream 2020—Miffs Users by Halting Work on the Enterprise Switch," *Communications*

Week 618, 8 July 1996, www.techweb.com/se/directlink
.cgi?CWK19960708S0005.

10. Lach.

11. Jackson-Higgins.

12. Monua Janah, "The Rules According to Cisco—Amid a Buying Spree, the Company Is Pushing Its Networking Software as the Industry Standard," *Information Week,* 16 September 1996, www.techweb.com/se/directlink.cgi?IWK19960916S0018.

13. Jackson-Higgins.

CHAPTER 5

1. Cecily Barnes, "Why Go Home?" *MetroActive,* 28 August 1997.

2. Dominic Bencivenga, "Employers and Workers Come to Terms," *HR Magazine,* June 1997.

3. Joe Flower, "The Cisco Mantra," *Wired,* March 1997, www
.wired.com/wired/archive/5.03/ff_cisco_pr.html.

4. Cisco Systems Profile, 30 October 1999, www.vaultreports
.com.

5. Pamela Kruger, "Make Smarter Mistakes," *Fast Company,* October 1997, www.fastcompany.com/online/11/mistakes.html.

6. Cisco Systems Profile.

7. Emory Thomas Jr., "Drink Beer, Get Free Stuff—Get Hired," MSNBC, 1 July 1999, www.zdnet.com/zdnn/stories/news/
0,4586,2286811,00.html.

8. Barnes.

9. Cisco Systems Profile.

10. Michelle V. Rafter, "Point System," *Industry Standard,* 28 June 1999.

11. Rajiv Chandrasekaran, "In Silicon Valley, a Computer Talent Hunt by Air and Internet," *Washington Post,* 30 November 1997, p. A21.

12. Bencivenga.

13. Robert X. Cringely, "It Beats Flipping Burgers: How Cisco Systems Is Using High School Students to Dominate the Internet," *PBS Online,* 3 June 1999. www./pbs.org/cringely/.

14. Scott Kirsner, "Nonprofit Motive," *Wired,* November 1999, www.wired.com/wired/archive/7.09/philanthropy.html.

CHAPTER 6

1. Anonymous, "Take It from the Top: An Interview with John Chambers," 9 September 1996, www.nwfusion.com/news/1997/1006chambers.html.
2. Luc Hatlestad, "Routing the Competition," *Red Herring,* March 1997, www.redherring.com/mag/issue40/routing.html.
3. Joe Flower, "The Cisco Mantra," *Wired,* March 1997, www.wired.com/wired/archive/5.03/ff_cisco_pr.html.
4. Andy Reinhardt, "Cisco: Crunch Time for a High-Tech Whiz," *Business Week,* 28 April 1997, www.businessweek.com/1997/17/b3524136.htm.
5. Jeff Caruso, "Missteps Don't Interrupt Cisco's Momentum, *InternetWeek,* 8 December 1997, www.internetwk.com/news/news1209-1.htm.
6. Kevin Tolly, "Lack of Commitment Could Doom NIA," Tolly Group.Home Page, www.tolly.com/kt/NWW/columns/970609NIA.html.

CHAPTER 7

1. Kimberly Caisse, "Cisco Routes Rivals with Tech Support," *Computer Reseller News Special Reports,* November 1999, www.crn.com/sections/special/supplement/847/847cc25.asp.

CHAPTER 8

1. Laura M. Holson, "Whiz Kid: Young Deal Maker Is the Force behind a Company's Growth," *New York Times on the Web,* 19 November 1998, www.cisco.com/warp/public/750/acquisition/articles/volpi.html.
2. Holson.
3. Anonymous, "Cisco's Vision of the Future," *InnovationNews,* September 1998, www.innovationmall.com/CiscoCEO.htm>.
4. "Remarks by the President and the Vice President at Electronic Commerce Event," 30 November 1998, www.npr.gov/library/speeches/rmkselec.html.

5. John O'Hanlan, "Cisco Systems—S. VP—Interview," *Wall Street Corporate Reporter,* 12 February 1999, p. 3

6. Joe Flower, "The Cisco Mantra, *Wired,* March 1997, www.wired .com/wired/archive/5.03/ff_cisco_pr.html.

CHAPTER 9

1. Andrew Kupfer, "The Real King of the Internet CEO John Chambers Wants to Make Cisco a Telcom Dynasty, but Lucent and Nortel Are in His Way," *Fortune,* 7 September 1998.

2. Cassimir Medford, "House's Vision for Nortel Networks—His View of the Network of the Next Century Goes from Adaptive to Omnipresent," *VARBusiness,* 26 October 1998, www.techweb .com/se/directlink.cgi?VAR19981026S0025.

3. Jeffrey Young, "The Next Net," *Wired,* April 1999, www .wired.com/wired/archive/7.04/cisco.html.

4. Chuck Moozakis, "Users Dubious as Sprint Readies ION 2.0," *InternetWeek* 761, 19 April 1999, www.techweb.com/se/ directlink.cgi?INW19990419S0021.

Index